Praise for *Analytics: The Agile Way*

"These days, every company knows they need to embrace analytics—but all too often, they're doing it wrong. Read Phil Simon's new book to understand the path forward, and leverage the power of data in a faster, cheaper, better way."

—Dorie Clark, author of *Stand Out* and adjunct professor, Duke University Fuqua School of Business

"Most companies, especially the larger ones, are realizing that their data availability and data abilities will make or break them. Huge investments are being made into creating actionable analytics—that next level of data insight. Yet many continue to pursue analytics in a Waterfall, phase-gate approach that makes those insights late to the party. *Analytics: The Agile Way* contains the spot-on guidance that everyone involved needs to know about analytics, Agile methods, and their intersection."

—William McKnight, President, McKnight Consulting Group

"Quite obviously, the *value* of analytical insights that make it into practice is far more important than the *depth* of the analytics. Increasing that value may be *the* key challenge in the analytics space. Phil Simon's latest book provides some clues, adopting highly successful Agile methods to the cause."

—Tom Redman, Ph.D., "the Data Doc," and author of *Getting in Front on Data: Who Does What*

"The real focus of technology today is around new answers to previously unsolvable problems: analytics. Unfortunately, old methods of developing analytics, algorithms, etc., are just too slow, risky, and costly. Businesses need a fast, cheap way to prove (and then improve)

the worth of analytics. Phil explores the Agile approach to analytics and then backs it up with a number of case studies—many of which he helped developed. If you are unclear on how your firm should approach analytics, this book serves as the starting point."

—Brian Sommer, IT industry analyst and President,
TechVentive, Inc.

"Even for those who have been working with data for many years (like me), this is an eye-opening book."

—Michael Schrenk, competitive intelligence specialist and
author of *Webbots, Spiders, and Screen Scrapers*

"Phil Simon nails it. For more than a quarter century, high-impact business value from our efforts in analytics and business intelligence has been a hit-or-miss proposition. Today we have an entirely new generation of data management and analytics, and the approaches described in this book can help organizations pivot toward the best techniques—and an entirely new philosophy—to achieve the most from our new technology."

—Alan Simon, senior lecturer, Arizona State University

Analytics

Wiley & SAS Business Series

The Wiley & SAS Business Series presents books that help senior-level managers with their critical management decisions.

Titles in the Wiley & SAS Business Series include:

Analytics: The Agile Way by Phil Simon

Analytics in a Big Data World: The Essential Guide to Data Science and its Applications by Bart Baesens

A Practical Guide to Analytics for Governments: Using Big Data for Good by Marie Lowman

Bank Fraud: Using Technology to Combat Losses by Revathi Subramanian

Big Data Analytics: Turning Big Data into Big Money by Frank Ohlhorst

Big Data, Big Innovation: Enabling Competitive Differentiation through Business Analytics by Evan Stubbs

Business Analytics for Customer Intelligence by Gert Laursen

Business Intelligence Applied: Implementing an Effective Information and Communications Technology Infrastructure by Michael Gendron

Business Intelligence and the Cloud: Strategic Implementation Guide by Michael S. Gendron

Business Transformation: A Roadmap for Maximizing Organizational Insights by Aiman Zeid

Connecting Organizational Silos: Taking Knowledge Flow Management to the Next Level with Social Media by Frank Leistner

Data-Driven Healthcare: How Analytics and BI Are Transforming the Industry by Laura Madsen

Delivering Business Analytics: Practical Guidelines for Best Practice by Evan Stubbs

Demand-Driven Forecasting: A Structured Approach to Forecasting, Second Edition by Charles Chase

For more information on any of the above titles, please visit www.wiley.com.

Other Books by Phil Simon

Message Not Received: Why Business Communication Is Broken and How to Fix It

The Visual Organization: Data Visualization, Big Data, and the Quest for Better Decisions

Too Big to Ignore: The Business Case for Big Data

The Age of the Platform: How Amazon, Apple, Facebook, and Google Have Redefined Business

The New Small: How a New Breed of Small Businesses Is Harnessing the Power of Emerging Technologies

The Next Wave of Technologies: Opportunities in Chaos

Why New Systems Fail: An Insider's Guide to Successful IT Projects

Analytics

The Agile Way

Phil Simon

WILEY

Cover image: Phil Simon/Wiley
Cover design: Wiley

Published by John Wiley & Sons, Inc., Hoboken, New Jersey.
Published simultaneously in Canada.

For general information on our other products and services or for technical support, please contact our Customer Care Department within the United States at (800) 762-2974, outside the United States at (317) 572-3993, or fax (317) 572-4002.

Wiley publishes in a variety of print and electronic formats and by print-on-demand. Some material included with standard print versions of this book may not be included in e-books or in print-on-demand. If this book refers to media such as a CD or DVD that is not included in the version you purchased, you may download this material at http://booksupport.wiley.com. For more information about Wiley products, visit www.wiley.com.

Library of Congress Cataloging-in-Publication Data

Names: Simon, Phil, author.
Title: Analytics : the agile way / Phil Simon.
Description: Hoboken, New Jersey : John Wiley & Sons, 2017. | Series: Wiley & SAS business series | Includes bibliographical references and index. | Identifiers: LCCN 2017020140 (print) | LCCN 2017026344 (ebook) | ISBN 978-1-119-42420-8 (pdf) | ISBN 978-1-119-42419-2 (epub) | ISBN 978-1-119-42347-8 (cloth) | ISBN 978-1-119-42421-5 (obook)
Subjects: LCSH: Business intelligence—Data processing. | Decision making.
Classification: LCC HD38.7 (ebook) | LCC HD38.7 .S535 2017 (print) | DDC 658.4/033—dc23
LC record available at https://lccn.loc.gov/2017020140

Printed in the United States of America.

10 9 8 7 6 5 4 3 2 1

The readiness is all.

—Hamlet

Contents

Preface

The Power of Dynamic Data

> *The most valuable commodity I know of is information.*
>
> —Michael Douglas as Gordon Gekko, *Wall Street*

O n August 7, 2015, the mood at Chipotle headquarters in Denver, Colorado, was jovial. The stock (NYSE: CMG) of the chain of "fast casual" Mexican restaurants had just reached an all-time high of $749.12. Sure, the company faced its fair share of challenges (including an alarmingly high number of lawsuits), but today was a day to celebrate.

Fast-forward six months. As so often is the case these days, things had changed very quickly.

A series of food-borne illnesses came to light at the end of 2015— and not just a few mild stomachaches caused by a batch of bad salsa. The true culprit: *E. coli*. As the Centers for Disease Control and Prevention (CDC) announced on December 2, 2015, "52 people from nine states have been sickened, 20 have been hospitalized, and there are no deaths."[1]

By April 16, 2016, Chipotle's stock was in free fall, dropping 40 percent from its high to $444. Things continued to spiral downward for the chain. The stock hit $370 on December 9 of that year. In August 2016, nearly 10,000 employees sued the company for unpaid wages. In September, a 16-year-old girl won a $7.65 million lawsuit against the company for sexual harassment. One of the victim's attorneys described the situation as "a brothel that just served food."[2] Damning words to be sure.

Sensing opportunity, activist investor Bill Ackman started gobbling up Chipotle equities. His hedge fund, Pershing Square Capital Management (PSCM), purchased large quantities of options trades, "normal" stock buys, and equity swaps. Rumor had it that Ackman wasn't just looking to make a buck; he wanted seats on the Chipotle board and a significant say in the company's long-term and daily management. And PSCM wasn't the only hedge fund betting long on CMG in 2016. Plenty of others were taking notice.[3]

Ackman is an interesting cat and a mixed blessing to the Chipotles of the world.* Over the years, he has earned a reputation as a thorn in the side of many distraught companies and their boards of directors. Still, Chipotle executives knew that his hedge fund was keeping their portfolios healthy. No doubt that CMG would have fallen further if PSCM and other funds weren't buying so aggressively.

Why were hedge funds buying Chipotle's shares on the cheap in 2016? You don't need to be Warren Buffett to see what was happening. The heads of these funds believed in the long-term value of the stock. Chipotle would eventually recover, they reasoned, so why not make a few bucks? In a way, Ackman and his ilk are no different from Homer Simpson. The patriarch of the iconic cartoon family once summarized his remarkably facile investment philosophy in the following seven words, "Buy low. Sell high. That's my motto."†

This begs the natural question: On what basis do these folks make their multibillion-dollar bets?

At a high level, sharks such as Ackman operate via a combination of instinct and analysis. With regard to the latter, hedge funds have always coveted highly quantitative employees—aka *quants*. As Scott Patterson writes in *The Quants: How a New Breed of Math Whizzes Conquered Wall Street and Nearly Destroyed It*, their complex and proprietary models factor in dozens or even hundreds of variables in attempting to predict stock prices and place large wagers.

New and unexpected data sources could be worth a fortune.

---

* Watch an interview with him on *Charlie Rose* at http://bit.ly/2mTzWKv.
† From "Burns Verkaufen der Kraftwerk," one of my very favorite episodes of *The Simpson*.

FOURSQUARE'S RISE, FALL, AND DATA-DRIVEN SECOND ACT

Although Facebook beat it by five years, Foursquare still arrived relatively early at the social-media party. Launched in March 2009 as a "local search-and-discovery service mobile app," it didn't take long for the company to approach *unicorn* status. Cofounder and CEO Dennis Crowley became a bona fide rock star. Millions of people used the app to check in to restaurants and bars. Of course, none of this would have been possible as late as 2006. By 2009, though, the smartphone revolution was in full swing. Foursquare could piggyback on the ubiquity of iPhones and Droids.

Crowley and Foursquare allowed anyone to download and use the app for free. Millions of people did. Oodles of active users, however, do not a business model make. There's a world of difference between a *user* and a *customer*.

At some point, like all enterprises, Foursquare needed to make money. By growing its *user* base, Foursquare hoped to expand its *customer* base: local businesses that could create highly targeted ads that its millions of users would see and, it was hoped, act on.

Foursquare was about to take location-based advertising into the smartphone age. No longer would a city pub owner or restaurateur need to pay someone to interrupt passersby on the street and hand out cards that advertised two-for-one drink specials. Via Foursquare, eateries could reach potential customers in a way never before possible.

At least that was the theory.

Foursquare's promise has always exceeded its financial results. For all of its users and hype, the company has never reported earning a profit.[4] At different points in 2012, both Marissa Mayer's acquisition-happy Yahoo! and Facebook reportedly flirted with acquiring Foursquare. In the end, though, the parties never consummated a deal.[5] Yahoo! remained a mess, and Facebook didn't really need Foursquare. Its network was enormous, and it wasn't as if the idea of a *check-in* had never occurred to Mark Zuckerberg. (In August 2010, the social network launched Places, a feature "not unlike" Foursquare.[6]) Determined to remain relevant, Crowley and his troops soldiered on.

Version 2.0: Two Apps Are Better Than One

On May 15, 2014, Foursquare launched a spin-off app called Swarm. The new app allowed users to broadcast their locations to their friends on social networks such as Facebook and Twitter. The main Foursquare app would still exist, but with a new focus. It would attempt to wean market share from Yelp. Writing for *The Verge*, Ben Popper and Ellis Hamburger explained the two apps' different purposes:

> Swarm will be a social heat map, helping users find friends nearby and check in to share their location. The new Foursquare will ditch the check-in and focus solely on exploration and discovery, finally positioning itself as a true Yelp-killer in the battle to provide great local search.[7]

Splitting Swarm from the Foursquare app has not turned out to be a panacea. Over the past few years, many industry analysts have doubted its long-term financial solvency. Foursquare has lost its status as an *it company*. In Figure P.1, Google Trends shows just how far the company has fallen.

Something had to give.

On January 14, 2016, COO Jeff Glueck replaced Crowley as CEO. On the same day that that long-rumored change of leadership took place, Foursquare bit the bullet and announced a new investor lifeline at a fraction of its prior valuation. Yes, the company and its employees had to endure the ignominy of the dreaded *down round*. As Mike Isaac wrote for the *New York Times*:

> Foursquare said it had raised $45 million in a new round of venture funding, as it tries to bolster its location data-based advertising and developer businesses. The financing pegs Foursquare's valuation at *roughly half* of the approximately $650 million that it was valued at in its last round in 2013, according to three people with knowledge of the deal's terms, who spoke on the condition of anonymity.[8] [Emphasis mine.]

Despite Foursquare's well-documented struggles, the app still sports a reported 50 million monthly active users.[9] As Bloomberg TV's Cory Johnson is fond of saying, "That ain't nothin'." Was it possible that Foursquare's next and ultimately best business model was staring its management in the face?

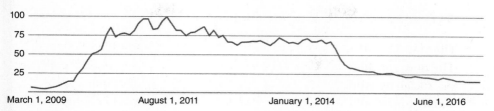

Figure P.1 Foursquare Interest over Time, March 1, 2009, to March 29, 2017
Source: Google Trends.

Version 3.0: A Data-Induced "Pivot"

On April 12, 2016, Glueck penned a fascinating post on Medium[10] that qualified as *bragging* or at least *posturing*. The Foursquare CEO revealed how his company collated user check-in data and other variables to accurately predict Chipotle's first-quarter sales. (The number dropped nearly 30 percent compared to the fourth quarter of 2015.)

As anyone who has studied retail knows, *foot traffic* isn't a terribly innovative concept these days. Brick-and-mortar retailers have known for many decades that it can serve as a valuable proxy for sales and revenue. All else being equal, there's a direct relationship between the former and the latter. Still, Glueck's lengthy data- and graph-laden article illustrated the power of "digital" foot traffic. Figure P.2 shows one of the post's charts.

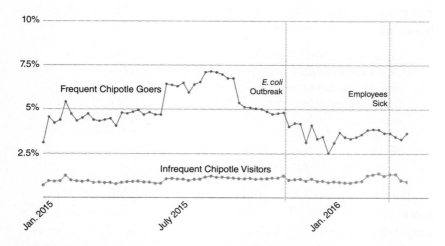

Figure P.2 Chipotle Share of Restaurant Foot Traffic (Week over Week)
Source: Foursquare Medium feed.

Glueck's post does not formally ask the following questions, but it certainly implies them:

- What if Foursquare could harness this type of data en masse and tie it to detailed user demographic information? (Foursquare allows its users to log in via Facebook, arguably the world's richest data trove.)
- Would companies with physical presences be willing to pony up for this kind of information? (Better question: Why *wouldn't* they be willing to pay handsomely for it?)
- What about opportunistic hedge-fund managers looking to outsmart the market? What about the Bill Ackmans of the world?
- Could Chipotle use location-based information to offer different deals and coupons to its growing number of ex-customers? Could Foursquare help Chipotle rescue customers? Could it be a means to an end?
- Would any chain restaurants be willing to pay Foursquare *not* to release this type of damning information? (Admittedly, this might qualify as *blackmail* or at least as *unethical*.)

Glueck wasn't just speculating about what his company could theoretically offer. As it turns out, Foursquare no longer just sells in-app ads to local bars and restaurants; an unknown but evidently increasing revenue stream for the company involves "renting" its data to interested parties. Foursquare's new Place Insights service purportedly offers:

- Insights from the world's largest opt-in foot traffic panel
- Overnight analysis of a global, cross-category dataset
- Translation of real-world behavior into business health, trend detection, and consumer insights*

Put differently, Glueck is attempting to redefine Foursquare as a data-licensing company. Just look at the company's website copy in early 2010:

> Foursquare on your phone gives you & your friends new ways of exploring your city. Earn points & unlock badges for discovering new things.†

---

* See https://enterprise.foursquare.com/insights.
† See http://bit.ly/2oImTsS.

The focus is clearly on the consumer/user. At the time, many companies employed gamification strategies. Now contrast that one with the company's business-first message today:

> Foursquare is a technology company that uses location intelligence to build meaningful consumer experiences and business solutions.*

The differences between Foursquare's early message and its contemporary one could not be more stark. Nothing against Joe Sixpack or Melissa Millennial, but they probably don't understand what *location intelligence* and *meaningful consumer experiences* even mean. I doubt that they would sign up for them. It's a moot point, though, because Foursquare isn't chasing the Joes and Melissas anymore. They don't pay the bills, at least directly.

Given Foursquare's history, its decision to rebrand is no coincidence, nor is its new message isolated to its website. Foursquare now consistently refers to itself as a "location intelligence company." Just view its official Twitter† and Medium‡ feeds. Its blog posts, while certainly informative, are meant to plant a very specific seed in the heads of prospective customers—that is, firms that would benefit from using Foursquare's data. For instance, in a post on Medium dated August 4, 2016, Foursquare claimed that it knew precisely how many women (justifiably) avoided Trump properties during the 2016 presidential election.§ Other posts boast previously successful predictions of Apple iPhone 6 sales and the impact of the decision by McDonald's to sell breakfast all day long.

To use Eric Reis's now-hackneyed term, if Foursquare successfully *pivots*, it would be neither the first in history nor the craziest. YouTube began as "Tune In Hook Up," a dating site redolent of HotorNot.** Instagram used to be Burbn, a location-based gaming and social networking app nearly identical to Foursquare.[11] Before finding its footing with photos, Flickr focused on gaming.

---

* See https://foursquare.com/about.

† See https://twitter.com/@foursquare.

‡ See https://medium.com/@foursquare.

§ See http://bit.ly/2lOtPaE.

** See http://mashable.com/2011/02/19/youtube-facts.

Chapter 3 will return to Foursquare in the context of streaming data and application program interfaces. For now, suffice it to say that the current, data-oriented incarnation of Foursquare seems closer than ever to finally capitalizing on its promise.

CHAPTER REVIEW AND DISCUSSION QUESTIONS

- Foot traffic has always mattered. What's different about it today?
- Why would hedge funds and even individual investors be interested in data related to "digital" foot traffic? Can you think of any other uses for this data?
- Why has Foursquare struggled to meet its financial goals? What is it trying to do to finally meet them? Do you think that the company will succeed?

NEXT

Do stories, ideas, questions, and issues such as these interest you? Do you wish that you could use data and analytics in this way? If so, then keep reading. You have found the right book.

NOTES

1. "CDC Update: Chipotle-Linked *E. Coli* Outbreak Case Count Now at 52," *Food Safety News*, December 4, 2015, http://bit.ly/2na5c8C.
2. Virginia Chamlee, "Teen Chipotle Worker Wins $7.65M in Sexual Harassment Suit," *Eater*, September 29, 2016, http://bit.ly/2mMEstY.
3. John Maxfield, "Hedge Funds Gobbled Up Chipotle's Stock Last Quarter," *The Motley Fool*, February 25, 2017, http://bit.ly/2nq54h7.
4. Matthew Lynley, "How Foursquare Hopes to Hit Profitability," *Tech Crunch*, May 9, 2016, http://tcrn.ch/2naP2f1.
5. Alyson Shontell, "Remember, Dennis Crowley Could Have Sold Foursquare for $120 Million," *Business Insider*, January 11, 2013, http://read.bi/2mTtgMn.
6. Ryan Singel, "Facebook Launches 'Check-In' Service to Connect People in Real Space," *Wired*, August 18, 2010, http://bit.ly/2mvAraS.
7. Ben Popper and Ellis Hamburger, "Meet Swarm: Foursquare's Ambitious Plan to Split Its App in Two," *The Verge*, May 1, 2014, http://bit.ly/1hh0Dvd.

8. Mike Isaac, "Foursquare Raises $45 Million, Cutting Its Valuation Nearly in Half," *New York Times*, January 14, 2016, http://nyti.ms/2md5S9c.

9. Ken Yeung, "Foursquare Users Have Checked In over 10 Billion Times," *VentureBeat*, September 13, 2016, http://bit.ly/2mP7Wbx.

10. Jeff Glueck, "Foursquare Predicts Chipotle's Q1 Sales Down Nearly 30%; Foot Traffic Reveals the Start of a Mixed Recovery," *Medium*, April 12, 2016, http://bit.ly/2ngij51.

11. Megan Garber, "Instagram Was First Called 'Burbn,'" *The Atlantic*, July 2, 2014, http://theatln.tc/2ohL9BI.

Figures and Tables

Item	Description
Figure P.1	Foursquare Interest over Time, March 1, 2009, to March 29, 2017
Figure P.2	Chipotle Share of Restaurant Foot Traffic (Week over Week)
Table I.1	Project Plan for Launch of Generic BI Application
Figure 1.1	Data-Storage Costs over Time
Figure 1.2	The World's Most Valuable Companies by Market Cap as of July 29, 2016, at 10:50 a.m. ET
Table 2.1	Sample of Structured Data from Fictional Employee Table
Table 2.2	Affiliate Payments from GMC
Figure 2.1	Tweet about Data Scientists
Figure 2.2	Write and Rant Facebook Post
Figure 2.3	Initial Results of Cover Poll for *Analytics: The Agile Way* Cover Vote
Figure 2.4	*Data Roundtable* Front Page as of December 16, 2016
Figure 2.5	Results of Web Scraping via import.io
Figure 2.6	Page Views by Author on *Data Roundtable*
Figure 2.7	Simple CSV Example
Figure 2.8	Simple JSON Example
Figure 2.9	Simple XML Example
Figure 3.1	Google Trends: Analytics versus Key Performance Indicators (March 7, 2007, to March 7, 2017)
Table 3.1	Reporting versus Analytics
Table 3.2	Lleyton Hewitt's 2001 Performance versus Top 50 and Top 10 Players
Table 3.3	Traditional Analytics versus Event-Stream Processing
Figure 4.1	Agile Methods: Before and After
Figure 5.1	Simple Visual of Scrum Team Makeup
Figure 5.2	Relationship between Product and Sprint Backlogs
Figure 5.3	Schedule for a One-Week Sprint

(*Continued*)

Introduction

It Didn't Used to Be This Way

> *The value of an idea lies in the using of it.*
>
> —Thomas Edison

So how did Foursquare predict Chipotle's sales for the first quarter of 2016 with such scary accuracy?

Permit me four answers to this question.

Here's the *really* short one: data.

Here's the second, just-plain-short one: Foursquare collected accurate and real-time data on Chipotle check-ins over time. Equipped with this information, the company's data scientists built a model. That's it.

Now, I don't mean to oversimplify or to diminish Foursquare, its employees, or what it was able to do here. As explained in the preface, Foursquare merely answered a question by using the technology and data available to it with a considerable tip of the hat to:

- The hardware of third-party smartphone manufacturers such as Apple, Samsung, and others.
- Powerful software such as iOS and Android.
- Related tools in the form of software development kits and application program interfaces.

- The massive investments of Verizon, AT&T, and others to build their carrier networks.
- Government research and infrastructure projects.*

That is, Foursquare built something very impressive, but not entirely unprecedented—at least in today's environment—and not without considerable assistance. Jeff Bezos of Amazon has made the same point: Yes, he worked very hard, but his company did not need to build a national transportation system. It merely took advantage of the existing one.†

The third and longer answer is: I'm not exactly sure. Like all but a few people, I can't tell you *precisely* how the company worked its magic. For all sorts of valid reasons, Foursquare doesn't make its code base and user data freely available to the general public.‡ It's not an open-source project à la Atom, Github's "hackable text editor." I don't know Foursquare's technical specifications, nor have I studied the ins and outs of its application program interface.§ Finally, if I asked anyone in the know at Foursquare to fill me in, I wouldn't get very far. Why tell me? Ex-employees in the know have most likely signed nondisclosure agreements, anyway.

The fourth and final answer is concurrently both more ambiguous and more definitive. Without fear of accurate contradiction, I can tell you that Foursquare derived these insights by *not* following the path of so many of its predecessors.

A LITTLE HISTORY LESSON

Many companies have historically attempted to glean insights very methodically. Large and midsized firms in particular would slowly build and integrate their enterprise systems, data warehouses, data lakes, and data marts. As for small businesses, their owners typically had neither the time nor the expertise to cobble together data from a

---

* Many people are quick to point out government's flaws, but reluctant to acknowledge successes such as the ARPANET, the predecessor to the modern-day Internet.
† For a fascinating interview with the man, see https://charlierose.com/videos/29412.
‡ Nor do many of the companies profiled in this book.
§ Here's the starting point: https://developer.foursquare.com.

bunch of disparate sources. Even if they did, most couldn't afford the six- or even seven-figure price tags of software vendors' best-of-breed solutions.

For instance, consider a typical project plan for a new business intelligence (BI) application in 2002. It typically involved the steps and approximate time frames listed in Table I.1.

Table I.1 Project Plan for Launch of Generic BI Application

Phase	Description	Start Date	End Date
1	Evaluate proposals from software vendors, check references, and perform general due diligence.	2/1/02	5/31/02
2	Select winning bid. Negotiate terms and sign contract.	6/1/02	7/31/02
3	Extract data from legacy systems, clean up errors, and deduplicate records.	8/1/02	8/31/02
4	Implement and customize software, typically with help of expensive consultants.	9/1/02	10/31/02
5	Train users on new application.	11/1/02	2/28/03
6	Load purified data into BI application and address errors.	3/1/03	3/31/03
7	Launch application and squash bugs.	4/1/03	4/30/03
8	Engage vendor in on-site or remote application support.	5/1/03	6/30/03

Source: Phil Simon.

Think about it: More than a year would pass from the project's formal kickoff until employees actually used the application in a production environment—*and that's if everything went according to plan.* As I wrote in *Why New Systems Fail*, more than half of the time that doesn't happen. On the contrary, these types of projects routinely exceed their budgets (often by ghastly amounts), take longer than expected, don't deliver required or expected functionality, or experience some combination of all of these.

There are terms for these types of traditional, rigid, and ultimately unsuccessful information technology (IT) projects: *phase-gate* or *Waterfall*. In a nutshell, a new phase or stage cannot begin until the team has completed the prior one. You don't need to be a certified project manager professional to see the limitations of this approach, outlined in Table I.1.

For instance, what if the people gathering the business requirements miss a few key ones? This is a massive problem. In 2014, the Project Management Institute (PMI) released its Pulse of the Profession report. PMI found that "37 percent of all organizations reported inaccurate requirements as the primary reason for project failure." Less than half of organizations possess the resources to properly manage their requirements. Astonishingly, only one-third of organizations' leaders consider them to be critical.[1]

Beyond that, other questions abound:

- What if a user fails to disclose an essential data source?
- What if a key employee leaves the company?
- What if there's a bug in the software?
- What if step 3 (data conversion, cleansing, and deduplicating) takes longer than expected? What if this isn't nearly as simple as the software vendor and/or consulting firm intimated?

The answer to each of these questions is the same: The project won't hit its date without some type of concession. Typically, these take the form of increased resources, reduced functionality, or new (read: postponed) deadlines.

Lest you think that the aforementioned scenarios are rare, I've seen all of them happen multiple times. In fact, Waterfall projects typically suffer from multiple issues at each phase. Their cumulative effects have resulted in untold billions in wasteful spending, high-profile lawsuits, and executives looking for new jobs.

But I'm going to give you the benefit of the doubt. What if you never experience the problems endemic to Waterfall projects? What if all employees on the project predict with eerie certainty how long their tasks take? Everyone is on board, and organizational politics doesn't impede the project's progress. Is the new BI application guaranteed—or even likely—to produce the kinds of lofty results that the software vendor promised before money changed hands?

What happens *when*—not if—the world just changes? One year or more represents an eternity, especially today. Put differently, no longer do just about all organizations and their leaders think of analytics in a virtually identical manner.

Prominent consulting firms have taken notice. To this end, they have begun offering "rapid deployment" options. For instance, on September 13, 2016, analytics company Teradata debuted something called Rapid Analytic Consulting Engagement. From the company's press release:

> Teradata (NYSE: TDC) . . . today announced RACE,
> or Rapid Analytic Consulting Engagement, an agile,
> technology-agnostic methodology that gives clients insight
> into the potential business value of analytic solutions before
> an investment is made. Teradata's process fully delivers on
> commitments in just six to ten weeks, rather than months.[2]

In point of fact, Teradata is hardly the only firm to realize the futility of yearlong engagements without any payoff in the near future. Irrespective of moniker, the futures of Agile methods and of analytics are inextricably intertwined.

ANALYTICS AND THE NEED FOR SPEED

In most mature organizations of certain sizes, the process of developing *any* analytics remains downright painful, let alone meaningful ones. These projects resemble death marches, and their existence couldn't be more inopportune. Never before has the world moved as fast as it does today.

To be sure, many people feel this way. You may, and I certainly do, but forget what we think and feel. Let's look at some data.

Celebrating the 25-year anniversary of the World Wide Web in March 2014, *The Economist* examined the increasingly rapid adoption of new technologies. From the article:

> It took only seven years from the first web pages in 1991
> for the web to be used by a quarter of the American
> population. That compares with 46 years for electricity,
> 35 years for the phone and 26 years for television. The
> web, just 25 years old, is still at the start of its life.[3]

In important and perhaps irreversible ways, the speed of both business and life has intensified considerably over the past 10 years.

For instance, up until fairly recently, the notion of a *flash sale* didn't exist. Ditto for viral videos and trending tweets. If you happen to see the front page of the morning's newspaper (remember those?), it's a good bet that you've already heard about the top stories. Thanks to the ubiquity of contemporary technology, all signs point toward these trends continuing for the foreseeable future.

■ SPEED AND STRATEGY

First-mover advantage has served some firms exceptionally well. Amazon is a classic case study. From its inception, Jeff Bezos eschewed profits for sales and scale. No one can credibly argue with his strategy and its results. Kozmo, Pets.com, and other dot-com start-ups squandered hundreds of millions of dollars when they should have followed leaner, more capital-efficient approaches.

Other firms have done well by following their peers quickly. Facebook was hardly the first social network. Many people forget that Goto.com pioneered the pay-per-click model for monetizing search engines, not Google. UPS carefully watches what rival FedEx does and learns from the latter's mistakes. UPS then creates similar offerings.

Examples abound of companies that waited too long to enter markets. Consider Bing in search, the very definition of an *also-ran*. Amazon's 2014 Fire Phone failed to gain any traction. For a more obscure example, consider Ello. Launched in March 2014, the company arrived at the end of the social network soiree. Despite its initial hype, Ello today is very much a niche product,[4] hardly the Facebook rival that it had imagined.

The point here is one management gambit or type of product launch isn't innately better than another. These brief examples prove that one size does not fit all. As I've said many times before, you don't need to be first, but you certainly can't be last.* Try launching a social network, search engine, or smart phone today. Good luck with that.

---

* http://bit.ly/2mSyKDJ.

How Fast Is Fast Enough?

The answer is neither simple nor universal. At the risk of sounding like a stereotypical consultant, it depends. Retailers need to precisely track inventory in the period around—and certainly during—Black Friday. Do they possess that same need during a slow Saturday in July? What about for a pharmaceutical company or a nonprofit?

As you're waiting in your doctor's office, you might think that relatively stable industries like health care don't require real-time analytics—and you'd often be wrong. As Google has shown, by aggregating search results, data can prevent the flu and even the spread of infectious diseases.[5]

Franz Kafka once said, "Better to have, and not need, than to need, and not have." Although he died nearly a century ago, that axiom is particularly relevant today. The ability to move quickly is more essential than ever—even if it's not necessary at a given time. For instance, for decades Cisco has had the capability to close its books at the end of every business day. This is no small feat for such a large enterprise. Does the company always do this? Of course not, but the ability to easily accomplish this feat can be absolutely invaluable for diagnosing problems, assessing profitability, and answering business questions before the end of a day, week, month, quarter, or fiscal year.

Let's return to the question: With regard to analytics, how fast is fast enough today? Before answering, consider the following queries that will help you address your organization's need for speed:

- How quickly do your employees act on currently existing numbers? Real-time analytics don't mean a hill of beans if an organization's employees never use data to make decisions.
- Are there perils to acting too fast? In the race for speed, are you losing time to reflect on what the data isn't telling you?
- Does your organization's culture tolerate failure? If you act faster, then you are able to benefit in key areas. At the same time, though, you are also likely to make more mistakes.

No one can give you a simple, all-encompassing answer to these questions—myself included. I can say, however, that traditional methods to obtain analytics are almost always far too slow.

Fortunately, there's good news. Many folks are waking up. They have realized that the Waterfall method simply cannot meet the demands of modern business and life. They are eschewing drawn-out

IT death marches. In their place, organizations are adopting Agile methods to further their analytics goals.

Automation: Still the Exception That Proves the Rule

In his 2015 book *Flash Boys*, Michael Lewis of *Moneyball* fame details how Wall Street firms are spending billions of dollars to lay fiber. No, they are not doing pro bono public-works projects; their motivations are far less benevolent. They are trying to shave a few milliseconds off the time required to trade securities and derivatives. This phenomenon goes by the name *high-frequency trading* (HFT). Make no mistake: HFT means big money. Beyond these sizable investments, hedge-fund managers have filed lawsuits against one another for poaching key employees who have intimate knowledge of these proprietary, complicated, and very profitable algorithms.

At their core, these algorithms make trades far faster than we humans can. Still, traffic in a slow lane can mean billions of dollars in lost profits. Those few milliseconds can make all the difference.

Along these lines, *programmatic ad buying* refers to the increasing use of sophisticated software that automatically purchases digital advertising based on a panoply of rules. The days of slick presentations by Don Draper of *Mad Men* appear to be waning. Writing for digital-marketing agency Digiday, Jack Marshall noted:

> It's impossible to tell what portion of advertising is now
> traded programmatically, but it's definitely on the rise.
> Some agencies now say they're eager to buy as much
> media as possible through programmatic channels, and
> some major brands have even built out in-house teams to
> handle their programmatic ad buying as they spend more
> of their marketing budgets that way.[6]

HFT and programmatic ad buying give plenty of policy wonks and everyday people pause about the future of jobs. Driverless cars are coming, and, in general, artificial intelligence (AI) continues to encroach on our lives. As Nicholas Carr manifests in his book *The Glass Cage*, this trend shows no signs of abating. More automation isn't necessarily a good thing for society.

Even instances in which humans have replaced machines haven't always gone smoothly. Consider Facebook. It has struggled for years in determining which information NewsFeed ought to present to its users and in which order. NewsFeed initially required people to select which stories its billion-plus users would see, but it was only a matter of time before Mark Zuckerberg would let its vaunted algorithm finally assume the reins. On August 29, 2016, Zuckerberg decided that it was time for machine to replace man. The social network unceremoniously canned its trending team. It didn't take long for its human-free algorithm to go "crazy."[7]

At least you can take some solace in the fact that AI represents the exception that proves the following rule: Despite the fascinating and often unexpected insights that they reveal, analytics and data generally do not make decisions by themselves. For the most part, human beings do. *At least for now*, we generally and actively decide what—if anything—we do when confronted with analytics. And it is here where the wheat separates itself from the chaff.

❷ TIP

Data and analytics rarely make decisions by themselves. People still matter, and they can routinely increase their odds of success by intelligently using data and analytics.

BOOK SCOPE, APPROACH, AND STYLE

I'm a big believer in the concept of *truth in advertising*. To this end, allow me to explain what *Analytics: The Agile Way* attempts to achieve and how the book attempts to achieve it.

At a high level, the following pages explore how firms are eschewing dated Waterfall or phase-gate methods to make sense out of vast amounts of data and an increasing array of data sources. They are turning to nimbler methods such as Scrum. More than ever, there's tremendous upside to using analytics to act quickly—and significant risks to waiting too long.

To achieve this goal, these pages cover quite a bit of ground. As I have in all of my books, I again will attempt to synthesize seemingly disparate business technology and events and trends into a cohesive narrative. *Analytics: The Agile Way* is no exception. Along these lines, expect far more practice than theory.

Breadth over Depth

By design, *Analytics: The Agile Way* is a multidimensional book. It does not explore all of the ins and outs of any one topic. For instance, consider the topic of Chapter 5: Scrum. A quick Amazon search reveals nearly 1,800 books on that subject alone. *Analytics: The Agile Way* doesn't purport to cover Scrum in nearly the same level of detail as many of those tomes.

And it doesn't stop there. You can find plenty of insightful books on just about all of the other subjects in this book: building statistical models, learning how to program in different languages, and developing a variety of analytics.* To varying degrees, *Analytics: The Agile Way* delves into these subjects. Those looking for an in-depth, 10-step process for using analytics to transform specific industries such as health care, however, will be disappointed.

This is a conscious choice and, because of it, I reference quite a few valuable texts, videos, blog posts, and articles. You can ignore the footnotes, notes, and bibliography if you like, but they are rife with informative and complementary resources. In other words, I hope that this book is a starting point to further exploration.

Methodology: Guidelines > Rules

Analytics: The Agile Way does not advocate *strictly* adhering to any one development method. Yes, Part Two introduces Agile methods (specifically Scrum) as well as a simple six-step framework for deriving analytics. Still, this does not mean that achieving success with data and analytics is tantamount to baking a cake. It's not.

---

* Amazon currently sells 166 books related to "healthcare analytics" alone.

To glean profound insights via data and analytics—especially when employing Agile methods—requires guidelines more than proper rules. To borrow from the title of the 2016 book by Ben Lindbergh and Sam Miller on applying analytics to baseball, the only rule is that it has to work. Different business problems, industries, environmental factors, budgets, employee skills, scenarios, and types of data often mandate wildly different approaches. A given technique in one context may be ill advised. In another, it may be completely appropriate and even necessary. What worked for Company A often does not work for Company B.*

Technical Sophistication

As I know all too well, poorly configured or antiquated systems directly impede firms' efforts to harness one of their most valuable assets: data. To keep this book at a manageable length, I largely omit the technical and often arcane side of enterprise data. Readers won't find much advice on data modeling, normalization, and warehousing.† Aside from the occasional recommendation, the same holds true for related and important subjects such as database schemas and design, master data management, enterprise architecture, and technical processes such as extract, transform, and load. Each of these meaty topics is certainly important. Anyone who doesn't believe that they affect enterprise data is sorely mistaken. Nevertheless, they lie outside of the scope of this book.

Vendor Agnosticism

On many levels, ours is a unique era. We have never had more data at our disposal—often an overwhelming amount flying toward us with increased speed. Data may or may not be "the new oil," but we cannot dispute its value *when used correctly*.‡ Ditto for analytics.

---

* Chapter 4 will return to this subject.
† If you want to know more here, see Ken Collier's *Agile Analytics: A Value-Driven Approach to Business Intelligence and Data Warehousing*.
‡ For my thoughts on the matter, see http://bit.ly/2naMMSc.

Fortunately, there have never been more ways to capture, buy, or rent this data. We can use powerful and affordable tools to analyze it, interpret it, and act on its insights. (Whether or not we do this remains to be seen.) Relatively new data-analysis programs, tools, and frameworks such as Tableau, R, Stata, D3, Hadoop, Hive, Pig, import.io, and countless others have exploded in popularity. Today, these accompany stalwarts such as Microsoft Access and Excel, SPSS, SAS Enterprise Miner and JMP, Minitab, and others.

Some of these tools are doubtless better suited for specific uses than others are. No one tool, programming language, or development framework can do everything. Still, this book is vendor-agnostic by design. It does not advocate any one software application over another. (Don't let the Teradata press release from earlier in the chapter fool you.)

The objectively "best" or "perfect" analytics tool—assuming that one even exists—will not guarantee successful results by itself. The firms and individuals best poised to find the signals in the noise need more than the latest tech and data tchotchkes. An Agile mind-set and a willingness to adapt quickly to changing circumstances are essential for little victories, never mind the big ones.

Yes, we'll cover examples of individual applications. By no means, though, am I implying that one is inherently better than another. Anyone looking for specific product recommendations will be disappointed, as will those seeking detailed application how-to guides and tutorials.

INTENDED AUDIENCE

More than ever, we need to do more than merely *understand* the insights that data can offer. We need to act on them. I wrote *Analytics: The Agile Way* for individuals interested in learning how to systematically turn data into something meaningful: analytics. More specifically, the book's intended audiences include the following four groups:

1. Undergraduate and graduate students new to the practice of analytics. (The questions at the end of each chapter are designed to provoke independent thought and in-class discussions more than supposedly correct answers.)

2. Functional users supporting different lines of business. These include entry-level analysts and senior executives. Many of these folks have only developed and deployed analytics in a more traditional manner.

3. Traditional analytics professionals who are rightfully curious about Agile methods.

4. Employees in technical fields who want to support their non-technical, internal clients better.

Regardless of your current role, though, if you're curious about trends in data and analytics and open to new ideas, then you should enjoy this book.

 ## A RECOMMENDATION FOR EMPLOYEES AT START-UPS

Analytics: The Agile Way is not geared toward a particular industry or company size. I like to think that its lessons apply irrespective of where you work. If you're looking for a book about the specific analytics challenges that start-ups face, check out *Lean Analytics: Use Data to Build a Better Startup Faster* by Alistair Croll and Benjamin Yoskovitz.

PLAN OF ATTACK

Analytics: The Agile Way consists of five parts. Part One (Background and Trends) lays the groundwork for the entire book. It describes the current data- and tech-centric business environment and how we arrived here. It also includes foundational chapters on data and analytics. After all, success begins with a common understanding of terms.

Part Two (Agile Methods and Analytics) begins with a short chapter on Agile principles. It then moves on to Agile methods with a particular focus on Scrum. It next introduces a simple six-step framework for Agile analytics that readers can apply to any number of analytics projects.

Part Three (Analytics in Action) provides windows into the analytics efforts of specific organizations. Here it's time for case studies. We'll see how progressive firms are rapidly and incrementally understanding their business problems—and developing solutions to them. That is, they have broken the inimical patterns that plague so many traditional analytics efforts.

Part Four ("Making the Most Out of Agile Analytics") takes a step back. It explores the lessons, benefits, and limitations of Agile analytics. You'll learn that the types of data and analytics available to you often hinge on product design. As such, Part Four concludes with a chapter on essential design considerations.

Part Five ("Conclusions and Next Steps") concludes the book. It asks some pointed questions about issues related to the growing use of Agile analytics. It covers new challenges with respect to data governance and data exhaust, privacy, and security.

CHAPTER REVIEW AND DISCUSSION QUESTIONS

- What are Waterfall or phase-gate projects?
- Do they lend themselves to successful outcomes? Why or why not?
- What are a few examples of automated decision making? Is this currently the exception or the rule? Do you expect that to change?

NEXT

Now that you know what this book covers and how, it's time to answer another big question: Why? The next chapter places analytics into a contemporary business context. It describes the major trends that have elevated analytics from optional to essential.

NOTES

1. Elizabeth Larson, "I Still Don't Have Time to Manage Requirements: My Project Is Later Than Ever," Project Management Institute, October 2014, http://bit .ly/2mjU6KR.
2. "Teradata Debuts Agile Analytics Business Consulting," September 13, 2016, http:// tinyurl.com/zna6lan.

3. "Happy Birthday World Wide Web," *The Economist*, March 12, 2014, http://tinyurl.com/jm2ltqw.

4. Charley Lock, "Remember Ello? You Abandoned It, but Artists Didn't," May 17, 2106, *Wired*, http://bit.ly/2eOhUmf, retrieved March 22, 2017.

5. Mary Chris Jaklevic, "Disease Sleuths Analyze Google Searches to Stop Infections," NPR, December 10, 2015, http://n.pr/1SQF742.

6. Jack Marshall, "WTF Is Programmatic Advertising?" Digiday, February 20, 2014, http://tinyurl.com/z37vql5.

7. Sam Thielman, "Facebook Fires Trending Team, and Algorithm without Humans Goes Crazy," *The Guardian*, August 29, 2016, http://bit.ly/2bMBfVv.

PART **ONE**

Background and Trends

P art One sets the stage for the rest of the book. It provides foundations in data and analytics on which the other parts build.

This part contains the following chapters:

- **Chapter 1:** Signs of the Times: Why Data and Analytics Are Dominating Our World
- **Chapter 2:** The Fundamentals of Contemporary Data: A Primer on What It Is, Why It Matters, and How to Get It
- **Chapter 3:** The Fundamentals of Analytics: Peeling Back the Onion

Signs of the Times

Why Data and Analytics Are Dominating Our World

Technology is eating the world.

—Marc Andreessen, August 20, 2011

O n August 20, 2011, the ex-Netscape founder and current rock-star venture capitalist uttered these five words—perhaps the most telling and quoted words of the Internet age. In a nutshell, technology has spawned powerful new companies and industries and decimated others. It has led to revolutions, unprecedented wealth, and new social mores and change that many institutions and individuals are barely beginning to process.

I am in the privileged position to have lived through all of this; consequently, I can wax poetic about things to which students probably cannot relate. (In a few of my books, I have done just that.) Yes, I remember getting my first e-mail as a sophomore at Carnegie Mellon in 1991. (I was blown away.) I too once thought that entering your credit card information into a computer was downright weird. I recall telephone booths, answering machines, flip phones, primitive web browsers, search results that weren't remotely accurate, when Napster was a thing, and nascent social networks such as Friendster that went down more often than they stayed up.

This is not a book about technology per se; it is a book about one of the most important consequences of ubiquitous technology: the explosion of data and the practice of analytics. Make no mistake: These are direct descendants of our tech-centric times. Absent the arrival of the World Wide Web, the smartphone explosion, cheap data storage, and the digitization of books, newspapers, songs, photos, and more, analytics and data wouldn't be nearly as critical as they are today. This chapter looks at those trends.

THE *MONEYBALL* EFFECT

Billy Beane attained fame in baseball and analytics circles long before Brad Bitt portrayed him in the 2011 film *Moneyball*. In fact, Beane was making quite the name for himself even prior to Michael Lewis's 2004 book of the same name.

It's no overstatement to claim that as general manager of the small-market Oakland A's, Beane changed the game of baseball forever. Big-market powerhouses such as the New York Yankees, Boston Red Sox, and Los Angeles Dodgers could effectively print their own money. Not Beane. He had to compete with a relatively paltry annual budget of roughly $60 million. That meant that he couldn't even dream of chasing other teams' pricey free agents. In fact, he had to let many of his own stars walk.* Case in point: Beane had no

---

* One of my favorite quotes from the movie: "The problem we're trying to solve is that there are rich teams and there are poor teams. Then there's fifty feet of crap, and then there's us."

shot of re-signing all-star first baseman Jason Giambi in 2001. The slugger and later admitted steroid user upped with the Yankees for nearly $120 million over seven years. Beane couldn't justify spending nearly 30 percent of his budget on a single player—no matter how prolific.

Instead, Beane proved that necessity is the mother of invention. He famously plucked players off other teams' scrap heaps, especially if they possessed odd skills. Player X can't hit home runs? No problem. Can he frustrate opposing pitchers by being "a tough out"? Can he just get on base? Beane drafted players who "just didn't look" like effective baseball players. His unorthodox methods angered many longtime Oakland scouts, men who had spent their careers watching players and developing a supposed eye for talent, not staring at spreadsheets. (The case study in Chapter 9 will have much more to say about resistance to analytics.)

You probably know how this story turns out. Would Michael Lewis write a book about you that turns into a movie starring Brad Pitt if you failed miserably? Pretty soon, even big-market teams such as the Yankees and Red Sox began hiring their own analytics experts, and later, *teams* of experts. The *Moneyball* movement spread beyond baseball to all other major sports. In fact, analytics are starting to move from the back room to the field. In their 2016 book *The Only Rule Is It Has to Work: Our Wild Experiment Building a New Kind of Baseball Team,* Ben Lindbergh and Sam Miller wrote:

> The Denver Broncos of the National Football League announce[d] that the team's director of analytics, Mitch Tanney, will break the front-office fourth wall in their upcoming games, speaking on a headset to head coach Gary Kubiak to offer his input on which plays the probabilities and percentages support. As managers increasingly come from cohorts that tend to be more perceptive to sabermetrics, it seems inevitable that something similar will happen in baseball.

Today, you'll find examples of *Moneyball* in areas and industries without any ties to sports at all. Case in point: the U.S. justice system.

In 2007, Anne Milgram became the attorney general of New Jersey. In her words, she "wanted to moneyball criminal justice."* Yes, *moneyball* is now a verb.

DIGITIZATION AND THE GREAT UNBUNDLING

Not *that* long ago, it was impossible to buy an individual song in a digital format. One could either hunt for the seven-inch 45 rpm record or just buy the CD—often at the exorbitant price of $15.99. The same held true for individual articles in newspapers and magazines, unless you wanted to read one at a newsstand.

Put differently, the Internet has created plenty of new industries, but disrupted or "unbundled" plenty of others. Writing for the *Harvard Business Review* in 2014, Justin Fox noted:

> Much of the business story of the digital age so far has been about taking products and institutions apart— unbundling them. Music CDs were unbundled into MP3s that were sold (and illicitly downloaded) individually. Newspapers have been unbundled by blogs and classified ad sites. Now, digital-education upstarts are trying to unbundle the university.[1]

And this trend has only intensified. In April 2015, HBO became the first cable network to offer its service independent of cable TV providers.† Dubbed HBO NOW, the service, for a flat monthly fee of $14.99, allows consumers to watch award-winning shows such as *Veep*, *Curb Your Enthusiasm*, and *Last Week Tonight* on their Apple TVs. No longer do customers need to buy pricey and wasteful cable packages from Verizon, Comcast, DIRECTV, and Cox Communications. Many industry analysts saw the move as an inevitable attempt to curtail piracy and lure tech-savvy cord-cutters and "cord-nevers" who consider the

---

* See Milgram's TED talk at http://bit.ly/2ndikqg.
† HBO announced the service at a much-ballyhooed Apple event in San Francisco at the Yerba Buena Center on March 9, 2015.

idea of paying $120 per month for a full-fledged cable TV subscription laughable. To goose subscriptions, HBO offered a free one-month trial to boot.

In several ways, this was a harbinger of things to come. HBO soon made its new service available on other "over-the-top" (OTT) devices such as Chromecast, Roku, and iOS and Android phones. It didn't take long for other cable TV channels to follow HBO's lead. Showtime Anytime launched on July 8, 2015, for $10.99 per month. In February 2017, AT&T fell in line with a similar offering for Starz and Starz Encore for $8 per month.

Now fans can legally binge-watch *Game of Thrones* at a fraction of what it would have cost two years ago.* Still, there's a more important benefit here. Think about the data implications of this move. Prior to launching HBO Now, the company did not maintain direct relationships with its customers. It needed to rely on intermediaries—in this case, cable companies—and pay for the privilege. Under the old model, HBO needed to compensate the Verizons of the world. Even worse, HBO could not directly and easily ascertain which shows its viewers were watching, when, and on which device. The cable networks can now do this—at least for their customers using apps via OTT devices. In other words, they can now do what Netflix has successfully done for years.

STEVE JOBS, THE *NEW YORK TIMES*, AND THE DATA WARS

Apple advocates customer privacy and often takes shots at Google/Alphabet for its "privacy-challenged" business model. As the following story demonstrates, though, it's folly to claim that Apple doesn't "get" the import of data.

(Continued)

---

*I am intentionally oversimplifying things here. For years, one could purchase individual seasons of popular shows via Apple's iTunes, Amazon's Prime Video, and other services. I gladly pony up $20 for seasons of AMC's *Better Call Saul*. In point of fact, I'd pay $20 per episode.

(*Continued*)

On April 3, 2010, Apple CEO Steve Jobs, to much hubbub, announced the launch of his company's latest game-changing product: the iPad. Consumers flocked to the device, although the product ultimately has not approached the iPhone's lofty sales figures. (As of November 2016, Apple had sold nearly 340 million iPads[2], making untold billions in the process.)

This was the first tablet that really mattered, and Jobs knew that he held tremendous power over potential partners. Not long after the launch, major media companies scurried to develop apps. In particularly cantankerous negotiations with the *New York Times*, Jobs insisted that Apple "own" the relationship with the customer and collect a fee for the privilege. That is, customers would subscribe to the *Times*'s new app either through Apple's app store or not at all.

Apple was flush with cash. It did not need a few dollars from the *Times*'s subscribers. This wasn't about money; it was about control and data. Jobs understood the cardinal importance of customer data, so much so that he was willing to anger an iconic newspaper and its loyal subscribers.

❓TIP

In business there have always been two ways to make money: to bundle and to unbundle. Right now we're living in an age of unbundling. In the process, data and analytics provide companies with an unprecedented opportunity to understand their customers, employees, products, and users.

AMAZON WEB SERVICES AND CLOUD COMPUTING

Up until 2006, most enterprises found it time-consuming and expensive to deploy new applications. Hardware and infrastructure vendors such as IBM largely charged their clients substantial installation and maintenance fees. Getting up and running was no small endeavor.

In 2006, one company started to change that.

Amazon launched a tiny experiment named Amazon Web Services (AWS). To run its core business, Amazon required powerful data centers, servers, and infrastructure, but even the e-commerce jugger-naut didn't use all of that capacity. Why let all of that excess compute power vanish into the ether? Why not rent its powerful infrastructure to companies as a service? It was a revolutionary and extremely prof-itable idea that the tech establishment didn't recognize until Amazon had built a sizable—perhaps even insurmountable—lead.

The AWS model did two critical things. First, it allowed companies of all sizes to *virtually* run their own applications, significantly reduc-ing deployment times in the process. Second, AWS did not charge its clients flat fees. Rather, costs varied in direct proportion to usage. In other words, its pricing model was flexible or elastic. This appealed to many CIOs whose IT budgets plunged in the wake of the 2008 finan-cial crisis. Organizations could now seriously consider whether they wanted to exit the IT business and "stick to their knitting." To this end, in 2008, Nicholas Carr penned the influential book *The Big Switch: Rewiring the World, from Edison to Google.* A century ago, most large companies produced their own electricity. Was a similar computing switch inevitable?

To call AWS *successful* is the acme of understatement. Amazon invented a multibillion-dollar product category. Its offerings currently go by clunky monikers such as Platform as a Service and Infrastructure as a Service. Although Amazon has spawned prominent imitators in the form of Microsoft, Google, and IBM, it continues to hold the pole position by a substantial margin. What's more, growth will continue for the foreseeable future. As Charles Babcock wrote on *Information-Week*, AWS

> continues to grow at a 50% per year pace. It's headed for
> $13 billion in revenues in 2017. In less than five years,
> it will be another $100 billion Amazon business if the
> current pace holds up.[3]

Lest you think that AWS appeals only to tiny start-ups searching for a business model, consider that the Central Intelligence Agency, Netflix, Airbnb, Zillow, and many other prominent organizations rely on Amazon. In the rare event of an AWS outage (such as the one that happened on March 28, 2017), people learn about it very quickly.

❷ TIP

More powerful, reliable, and affordable infrastructure means more business and consumer applications. This results in more data and—you guessed it—more analytics.

NOT YOUR FATHER'S DATA STORAGE

Up until fairly recently, data storage was both very expensive and very limited. Today, neither of those is true, and a brief history lesson will show just how far and fast we have come with those 1s and 0s.

How? Hadoop and the Growth of NoSQL

For a long time, organizations needed to store all of their data either in mainframes or in relational databases. (For decades, data storage was almost always on-premise.) These options haven't gone away. To be sure, many enterprises today continue to run smoothly with "back ends" such as Microsoft SQL Server, Oracle, and IBM's DB2. It's absurd to think, though, that these options represent the only or even the best way to store all types of enterprise data. Amazon has introduced a seismic shift in data storage and application deployment.

For starters, countless organizations have put their data "in the cloud."* Amazon Redshift and Microsoft Azure Data Lake are just two of the many cloud-based alternatives to storing data. Beyond *where* the data is stored, *how* it is stored may not look anything like it did in 1998. Distributed file systems such as Hadoop and popular NoSQL† databases such as Apache's Cassandra can yield significant advantages over their traditional and relational counterparts: Fault tolerance and parallel processing‡ are at the top of the list.

Brass tacks: Today, organizations face no shortage of flexible, powerful, and—as we'll see next—extremely affordable options for storing their data.

---

*I'm not a fan of this phrase because there is no one "cloud." For more on this, see http://bit.ly/2lLRZTh.
† Short for "not only SQL," not "no SQL."
‡ For more on this, see my book *Too Big to Ignore*.

How Much? Kryder's Law

In 2004, Google shocked the world by launching Gmail, a free e-mail service with one gigabyte (GB) of storage. This was a big deal. Today, Gmail offers 10 gigabytes of storage space for free accounts. Microsoft's free Outlook offers virtually unlimited storage.

All of this costs consumers zero. Ditto for basic accounts for Dropbox, Box.net, GoogleDrive, and Microsoft's OneDrive. None of these free services would exist if storage costs had not plummeted. As Figure 1.1 shows, they certainly have.

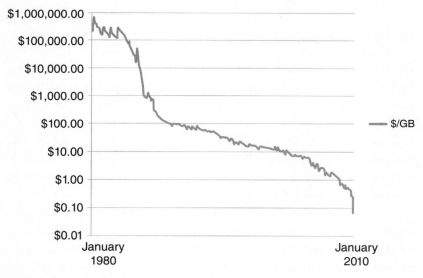

Figure 1.1 Data-Storage Costs over Time
Source: Data from Matthew Komorowski (see www.mkomo.com/cost-per-gigabyte) Figure from Phil Simon.

This phenomenon is known as Kryder's law. Not that long ago, data storage used to be terribly expensive for both enterprises and individuals. This has not been the case for a long time. Data storage is now orders of magnitude cheaper than it was in past decades.

❷ TIP

Cheaper storage and more powerful alternatives mean that organizations can store more data, and, by extension, develop more powerful and sophisticated analytics.

MOORE'S LAW

In 1965, Gordon Moore predicted that processing power for computers would double every 12 months.* At the same time, the cost of that technology would drop by half over the same time.

Although it cannot continue forever, Moore's law has held true for more than 50 years. It is the reason that if you own a contemporary smartphone, you hold in your hand more computing power than the Apollo 11 spacecraft that put the first man on the moon.

THE SMARTPHONE REVOLUTION

As a kid, I was scared of getting lost. I can remember losing track of my parents—or maybe it was vice versa—at a county fair when I was about 10 years old. I can remember someone announcing over the loudspeaker, "Will Philip Simon please come to the information booth?" Of course, I heard the announcement; it wasn't as if I was walking around listening to my iPhone or iPod.

I also remember my early trips on airplanes, some of which wound up delayed on the tarmac. When the pilot or flight attendant would announce that we weren't going anywhere for 15 minutes, the passengers and I would audibly moan.

Both of these scenarios are less likely to happen these days. Smartphones allow parents to call their children wherever and for whatever reason. Garden-variety travel delays don't seem to bother us as much as they once did. (Being physically removed from a plane, however, is another matter.) Most of us are oblivious to the outside world, dialed into our electronic devices. If we're listening to music, then we might not even *hear* those announcements in the first place.

The growth of smartphones—and to a lesser but nevertheless increasing extent, wearable technology—is absolutely staggering. In February 2017, Cisco reported that global data traffic from mobile devices "grew 63 percent in 2016" and reached "7.2 exabytes per month at the end of 2016, up from 4.4 exabytes† per month at the end of 2015."‡ Both

---

* For different reasons not worth discussing here, people often quote this as 12, 18, and 24 months.

† One exabyte is equivalent to 1 billion gigabytes and 1,000 petabytes.

‡ For the whole report, see http://bit.ly/1W26UQo.

actively and passively, we are generating more data than ever with no end in sight. To wit, an increasing amount of this data is *contextual*. That is, our smartphones can easily determine what we're doing when and where we're doing it (if we let them, of course). There's a reason that my iPad "recommends" that I open the YouTube app when I go to Lifetime Fitness and step on the treadmill. (I like to watch concert footage when I run. The news today just upsets me.)

THE DEMOCRATIZATION OF DATA

Let's go back in time to the 1984 Hackers Conference. The American writer and entrepreneur Stewart Brand said the following to legendary Apple cofounder Steve Wozniak:

> On the one hand information wants to be expensive, because it's so valuable. The right information in the right place just changes your life. On the other hand, information wants to be free because the cost of getting it out is getting lower and lower all the time. So you have these two fighting against each other.[4]

Brand was nothing short of clairvoyant. The trends described so far in this chapter reflect the fundamental conflict he referenced more than 30 years ago.

To be sure, not all information is free today. Many media sites have for years experimented with paywalls designed to protect their content from free riders. More recently, they have declared war on ad blockers. Music and movie piracy abound despite their industries' attempts to thwart them.

The tension between free and paid isn't going anywhere. For now, suffice it to say that "data" is more available, or, if you like, more *democratic* than ever. It's also much larger. After all, it's called *Big Data* for a reason. (Chapter 2 delves deeper into this subject.)

THE PRIMACY OF PRIVACY

In June 2015, Apple CEO Tim Cook spoke at the Electronic Privacy Information Center (EPIC) Champions of Freedom event in Washington, D.C. After being honored for excellent leadership in the area of privacy, Cook excoriated the companies that he felt were lagging in this regard:

> Like many of you, we at Apple reject the idea that our customers should have to make tradeoffs between privacy and security. We can and we must provide both in equal measure. We believe that people have a fundamental right to privacy. The American people demand it, the constitution demands it, morality demands it.
>
> Some of the most prominent and successful companies have built their businesses by lulling their customers into complacency about their personal information.[5]

Without naming names, no one could accuse Cook of being particularly subtle here. He was slamming Facebook and Google for what he believes are their cavalier stances on user privacy. Irrespective of Cook's unknown private opinions on the matter, his public stance certainly jibes with Apple's product philosophy. Apple doesn't need to monetize user data. Its high profit margins allow it to market "privacy as a feature," something that Microsoft has also adopted in recent years.[6]

Many consumers also report feeling this way. (It remains to be seen whether or not they vote with their wallets, though.) The public seems to be growing increasingly skeptical of what takes place online—and with good reason. From a 2014 Harris Interactive and TRUSTe study:

> . . . 84 percent of consumers are less likely to click on an online ad. Three-fourths are less likely to enable location tracking. In addition, a full 89 percent won't do business with a company that doesn't do a good enough job protecting them online. And 76 percent are likely to check websites and apps for a privacy certification seal.*

Companies that routinely ignore privacy concerns often face swift retribution and incur the wrath of their customers and users. Uber is arguably the poster child today, but it is hardly alone.

---

*Read the whole study here: http://bit.ly/2nEkrUb.

THE INTERNET OF THINGS

My friend Heather recently gave me a Nixplay Wi-Fi digital picture frame as a gift at my housewarming party. (Ironically, I had been thinking about getting one for a few months.) Within minutes, I connected it to my home network, installed the app on my smartphone and iPad, and started adding photos. It didn't take long before many of my favorite pictures appeared for my guests to see.

We're still in the early innings, but items such as these offer glimpses into a very connected future—specifically, the much-hyped Internet of Things. Make no mistake: It is coming, and not just for techies like me. As I wrote in a recent article for SAS, "Even traditionally conservative sectors such as farming stand to reap enormous rewards and savings in the form of greater crop yields, more efficient use of water, and the like."*

Cisco Systems has predicted that by 2020, 50 billion devices will connect to the Internet.† Even if that estimate is off by a factor of three, it's still an enormous number with obvious implications for data and analytics—to say nothing about security and privacy.

THE RISE OF THE DATA-SAVVY EMPLOYEE

Historically, a garden-variety marketing analyst didn't have to be a mathematical wunderkind. Today, though, that same entry-level analyst more likely than not knows her way around a spreadsheet. What's more, she's probably proficient with Google Analytics. The trend is unmistakable: Not only are employees increasingly tolerating working with data, but they are beginning to *demand* it.

Kathy Marshall serves as the director of recruitment quality and client engagement at Decision Toolbox, a recruitment products and services company. In her words:

> Data-savvy workers think differently, ask questions,
> challenge the establishment, and demand improvements.
> If a data-driven employee isn't challenged, can't affect

---

*Read the article at http://bit.ly/2mt8OB8.
†Read the white paper at http://bit.ly/1LgfMSb.

change, or isn't able to access the information they need to drive results, [they] will quickly move on to other opportunities.[7]

But what if you just don't "do numbers"? You're in trouble. It's getting harder for numerically challenged employees to find hiding places within organizations.

THE BURGEONING IMPORTANCE OF DATA ANALYTICS

On many levels, the trends described in this chapter have been nothing short of transformative. With regard to this book, they have individually, collectively, and *exponentially* increased the importance of data and analytics. These twins are more important than ever, but don't take my word for it.

Let's look at what happened on July 29, 2016.

A Watershed Moment

Lost in all of the hubbub of the most contentious presidential campaign of our lifetime, something remarkable and probably unprecedented happened on that summer day. For perhaps the first time in history, each of the five most valuable companies in the world (as measured by market capitalization) belonged to the technology sector. At least for a short while, Exxon, General Electric, and Johnson & Johnson took backseats to their tech-savvy brethren. Writing for *Slate*, Will Oremus noted:

> To be clear, this leaderboard in itself has no direct impact on, well, anything, other than public perception. No one gets a prize for ranking at the top of it, nor a penalty for dropping down the list. Still, it feels like a cultural moment to see what are sometimes called the "big five" U.S. tech companies surpass all others in market value.[8]

Figure 1.2 presents these companies' market capitalizations.

Fundamental differences certainly exist among these companies beyond a few hundred billion dollars in market cap. For instance, as mentioned earlier in this chapter, Amazon has aggressively expanded

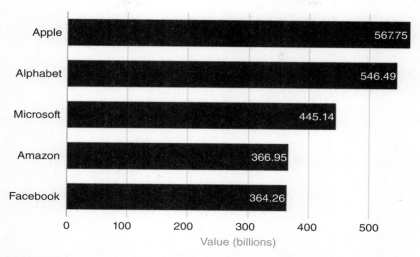

Figure 1.2 The World's Most Valuable Companies by Market Cap as of July 29, 2016, at 10:50 a.m. ET
Source: Data from Google Finance. Figure from Phil Simon.

its focus from its relatively humble beginnings. It's downright wrong—and has been for years—to think of Amazon as an online bookstore. Its cloud-computing division, AWS, generates more than $15 billion per year in revenue as well as the lion's share of the company's profits.[9]

For its part, Facebook has stayed largely true to its initial vision of making the world more open and connected. To this end, Mark Zuckerberg has made his fair share of high-profile acquisitions. By adding WhatsApp, Instagram, and Oculus, Facebook has cemented its position as the world's most popular and valuable social network. Unlike Amazon, Facebook has not made significant inroads into non-adjacent areas such as enterprise sales. (Facebook's recent efforts to hawk its new collaboration tool Workplace don't appear to be bearing much fruit.)

Common Ground

The cardinal similarity among these behemoths are data, and, by extension, analytics. Each company possesses incredibly large and valuable troves of customer and user information, although their strategies diverge considerably. Make no mistake: Amazon, Apple, and Microsoft may differ from Facebook and Alphabet/Google in how they treat privacy, but all five of these market leaders understand the import of data. Case in point: On June 13, 2016, Microsoft ponied up a mind-boggling $26.2 billion for professional social network LinkedIn. Many industry insiders consider the move to be nothing more than a large data grab.

CREATING CULTURES OF ANALYTICS

In September 2015, I gave the keynote speech at the JMP Discovery Summit in San Diego. The title of my talk was "How to Create a Culture of Analytics."* Over the course of an hour, I described how Netflix, Amazon, Facebook, and Google have institutionalized analytics in their organizations. To paraphrase the title of the book by ex-IBM CEO Lou Gerstner, it ain't easy, but some elephants can indeed dance.

And to these victors go significant spoils. Sure, these companies have succeeded for other reasons, including their competitors' missteps and dumb luck. Nevertheless, Wall Street likes what it has seen. Netflix, Amazon, Facebook, and Google have consistently outperformed their peers. On a personal level, I have found that as a general rule, organizations that embrace analytics and experimentation are able to move more nimbly compared to bureaucratic, data-agnostic organizations. They are less likely to suffer the fates of Blockbuster, Kodak, and other erstwhile powerhouses.

The Data Business Is Alive and Well and Flourishing

There's a reason that Facebook's stock is flying so high. Unlike Apple, a company decidedly not in the data business, Facebook has figured out how to monetize petabytes of user data. As we have seen, Wall Street has taken notice but, as always, isn't satisfied. The next logical step for Facebook is to open its vast data trove to those hungering for it the most. I'm talking here about the social network's *real* customers: its advertisers.† And Mark Zuckerberg is doing exactly that.

---

* Watch the talk at http://bit.ly/2moA5G8.
† If you use Facebook, then you are the product. Never confuse *users* with *customers*.

In 2013, Facebook purchased Microsoft's Atlas ad serving and tracking business for an estimated price of $100 million.[26] Relaunched by Facebook the following year, Atlas helps marketers and publishers at a high level:

- Load online ads into web pages and even individual apps.
- Measure which people their online ads are reaching.

For the past few years, Facebook limited the availability of some of its most promising ad products. Not anymore. Scott Shapiro currently serves as Facebook's product marketing director for measurement. "Previously, these tools were only available in Atlas for the largest enterprise marketers," he said in March 2017. "We're expanding the access of functionality that only existed in Atlas to tens of thousands of marketers who use Facebook's ad tools."[11]

Facebook clearly possesses something that scores of established companies want: incredibly detailed user demographic and psychographic data. Want to find female millennials in Manhattan who dig the HBO show *Girls*? No problem. Looking for male fans of the English prog-rock band Marillion who reside in London? Check. With nearly two billion users (many of them legitimate and routinely engaged), Facebook has advertisers frothing at the mouth. Atlas isn't exactly a hard sell.

ANTICIPATORY COMMERCE

For decades, Amazon has made it easy for millions of customers to quickly find what they want and place orders with a click of the mouse. Want to subscribe to toothpaste or even beef jerky? No problem. But what about fulfilling an order *before* you actually place it? That thought has occurred to Amazon as well.

In January 2014, word broke that Jeff Bezos's company had filed a patent for anticipatory commerce. As Greg Bensinger of the *Wall Street Journal* reported: "Amazon says it may box and ship products it expects customers in a specific area will want—based on previous orders and other factors. According to the patent, the packages could wait at the shippers' hubs or on trucks until an order arrives. If implemented well, this strategy has the potential to take predictive analytics to the next level, allowing the data-savvy company to greatly expand its base of loyal customers."[12]

Not Just the Big Five

Amazon, Facebook, Google, Microsoft, and—to a lesser extent—Apple are hardly alone in reaping outsize rewards from their early analytics and data-related efforts. Consider Netflix, a company that I discuss at length in *The Visual Organization*. I won't repeat myself too much here, but suffice it to say that Netflix knows a great deal about what its nearly 90 million subscribers are watching, when, and on which device. To put it mildly, detailed information on viewing habits informs the company's decisions on producing expensive original content—and leasing existing shows and movies. Netflix doesn't green-light shows willy-nilly. At roughly $5 billion in 2016 alone, content-acquisition costs represent one of Netflix's largest annual expenses.[13]

Uber: The Economist's Dream

Forget publicly traded companies for a moment. Uber, the world's richest *private* company at the time of this writing, sports a valuation of roughly $70 billion. Travis Kalanick's outfit knows far more about its customers and "driver-partners"* than most people realize. In fact, Uber's vaunted algorithm and app allow it to do things about which most CEOs can only dream.

If you have studied economics, you most likely learned about a concept called *consumer surplus*. Put simply, this represents the difference between the price that consumers are willing and able to pay for a good or service and the price that they actually pay (read: the market price). Let's say that you are really hankering for some blueberries. You go to your local grocery store and head to the fruit section. You would pay $5 for a carton of them. Fortunately, blueberries are on sale for $1. In this example, that $4 difference represents the consumer surplus.

Keeping with this example, it's practically impossible for your neighborhood Albertsons or Whole Foods to capture that $4. There's just no way for a store employee to effectively gauge how much each customer is willing to pay. That $1 price reflects a number of factors.

---

* For legal reasons, the company created this clunky term. By refusing to classify its drivers as *employees*, Uber saves billions in employee taxes and benefits. To be fair, many other "on-demand" companies do the same thing.

Perhaps there is an excess of blueberries and the store is "blowing them out" in lieu of tossing them out. Blueberries are perishable goods, after all.

Of course, Uber doesn't face this problem. Via data and its app, the company is able to offer dynamic and surge pricing. (Some would use the much less benign term *price gouging*.) In theory, surge pricing can match drivers and customers in real time. Remember that Uber's "driver-partners" are free to drive if and when they like. If Uber can't compel people to drive, then how can it meet consumer demand?

The answer lies in economics. Uber relies on market incentives to lure drivers out of their homes and onto the streets when its algorithm detects a dearth of them in a city. Uber automatically raises driver rates when customer demand rises. Put differently, nothing at Uber is fixed: not the per-mile rate, not the number of drivers, not the schedule. The same trip that cost you $15 last week might cost you twice that much today. It all hinges on supply and demand. For instance, consider New Year's Eve, typically a massive mismatch between supply of and demand for drivers. Over the course of Uber's history, many customers have taken to social media to vent about exorbitant rates on this day. After the ball dropped in Manhattan's Times Square in 2014, some inebriated riders were shocked to find that surge pricing resulted in fares six times higher than normal.[14]

Brass tacks: Uber is arguably able to capture more of the consumer surplus than any company in the history of modern-day capitalism. It may, in fact, be an economist's dream.* That's a far cry, though, from saying that it's all sunshine and lollypops for the ride-sharing juggernaut. It most certainly is not.

In 2014, the company faced a public maelstrom when word leaked that it was furtively employing "God View" tracking capability on unsuspecting customers. With a few clicks of a mouse, nosy employees could easily stalk celebrities, journalists, and rival ride-sharing exes.† The company ultimately settled a New York lawsuit.

---

* For more on this, see the *Freakonomics* podcast "Why Uber Is an Economist's Dream" at http://tinyurl.com/freakuber.

† To read the court documents, see http://tinyurl.com/uber-courtx.

Things have continued to go downhill for Uber. In a remarkable three-week period in March 2017, the company faced a string of PR nightmares, including:

- An ex-employee's viral blog post about the company's rampant harassment and discrimination.*
- A lawsuit from Alphabet (Google's parent company) over stolen intellectual property.
- A viral video in which Kalanick berated an Uber driver over fares.†
- A spate of executive turnover.
- A crash of a driverless car in Arizona and the subsequent suspension of its testing.
- Revelations that the company furtively developed technology designed to identify and circumvent government officials' efforts to detect if the service was operating illegally—aka Greyball.‡

April of 2017 didn't bode much better for Uber. Stories surfaced on its hyper-aggressive business practices, including illegally spying on Lyft drivers and tracking users' behavior after they had deleted the Uber app. (This practice, known as "fingerprinting," violates Apple's terms of service.)

Airbnb: Better (If Possibly Illegal) Living through Data

Next on the decacorn§ list is Airbnb, the disruptive and possibly illegal online marketplace and hospitality service. Its current private valuation is $30 billion. Much like at Uber, CEO Brian Chesky and his cofounders understand exactly what is happening on his company's "platform" at all times. Chesky et al. built Airbnb with data in mind from early on. As a result, Airbnb can easily answer questions such as:

- How many proper homes are available in Montreal right now? What's the average price per home, and how does that compare with available apartments?
- What was the average length of stay of Airbnb guests in New York last December? How did that change from the previous December?

---

* See http://bit.ly/2kX7hjw.
† See http://bit.ly/2mgAs2y.
‡ See http://nyti.ms/2nY3J54.
§ If *unicorns* are start-ups worth $1 billion, then *decacorns* are worth $10 billion.

- What is the trend in Paris? Are prices increasing or decreasing, and by how much?
- How many individual rooms are available in San Francisco? What about entire homes and apartments?
- How many hosts are violating local housing ordinances? (This may include listing multiple properties or listing properties for lengths of time outlawed by local statutes.)

Airbnb possesses an astonishing quantity and level of information on its customers and hosts—not that Chesky is keen on releasing that data to regulatory agencies, hotel lobbyists, affordable-housing activists, and others curious about whether the company is flouting the law. Under the guise of user privacy, Airbnb has routinely resisted calls to release its data. In fact, independent websites such as Inside Airbnb (insideairbnb.com) exist that seek to "add data to the debate." For more on this, see Brad Stone's excellent 2017 book *The Upstarts: How Uber, Airbnb, and the Killer Companies of the New Silicon Valley Are Changing the World*.

But it doesn't stop there. Airbnb aims to maximize customer recommendations and repeat customers—in this case, bookings. Like many companies, Airbnb uses Net Promoter Score (NPS), a customer-loyalty measure that dates back to 2003. At a high level, NPS asks one simple question: "How likely are you to recommend Airbnb?" In industry parlance, this is called *likelihood to recommend*. The company's data scientists methodically analyze and tweak the following variables:

- Overall review score and responses to review subcategories on a scale from 1 to 5
- Guest acquisition channel (organic or marketing campaigns)
- Trip destination
- Guest origin
- Previous bookings from the guest on Airbnb
- Trip length
- Number of guests
- Price per night
- Month of checkout (to account for seasonality)

- Room type (entire home, private room, shared room)
- Other listings owned by the host[15]

It may seem that Netflix, Uber, and Airbnb have built insurmountable leads via their extensive use of data and technology. For several reasons, though, that type of thinking is misplaced and shortsighted.

For starters, disruption happens faster than ever. Case in point: Up until the iPhone launched in 2007, the BlackBerry constituted nearly 40 percent of the cellphone market. On February 15, 2017, research firm Gartner reported that the BlackBerry's market share had plunged to 0.0 percent,[16] not that it has been remotely relevant for nearly a decade. Add to that the fact that *dominance* and *monopoly* are not synonyms. Hulu, YouTube, and Amazon are hot on Netflix's trail. Lyft is still a viable national ride-share alternative in the United States that continues to raise substantial funds.[17] (Some cities that have banned Uber and Lyft have endorsed smaller, local players that choose to abide by their rules. Ride Austin in Austin, Texas, is just one example.) Given Uber's burgeoning legal and PR troubles, success is anything but assured. And if you think that Airbnb is the only short-term rental marketplace around, you're mistaken.

DATA-RELATED CHALLENGES

This is not to say that today's powerful tech companies haven't struggled with data-related matters. Nothing could be further from the truth.

Facebook and Twitter received a great deal of valid criticism during and after the 2016 U.S. presidential election. Each social network failed to prevent or at least contain the spread of fake news. In one oft-cited example dubbed "Pizzagate," a North Carolina man "self-investigated" an apocryphal and politically charged story falsely claiming that Hillary Clinton was running a child-sex ring out of a pizzeria in Washington, D.C. As Joshua Gillin wrote on PolitiFact:

> Edgar Maddison Welch, a 28-year-old man from Salisbury, N.C., walked into Comet Ping Pong in the capital around 3 p.m. on Dec. 4. Police said he pointed his gun at a worker, who fled, and then Welch started firing the rifle inside the restaurant.[18]

While extreme, stories such as these on Facebook weren't uncommon during a most contentious election. In fact, the social network's algorithm creates these types of "filter bubbles," to borrow a phrase from Eli Pariser's remarkably insightful and prescient 2012 book. In March 2017, Facebook finally responded by adding a "mark as disputed" option to stories in its NewsFeed.* Many critics argued that the response was too little, too late. No argument here.

For its part, Amazon has filed several lawsuits against Fiverr, "a global online marketplace offering tasks and services, beginning at a cost of $5 per job performed." Amazon first took Fiverr to court in April 2015. Six months later, Amazon and its lawyers were back at it. The obvious question is: Why? As Sarah Perez wrote for TechCrunch:

> The defendants in the new case, listed as "John Does," each used Fiverr.com to sell fake positive or 5-star Amazon reviews. In some cases, they even offered "verified" reviews, meaning those where they buy the product— provided they're compensated for that, of course. Other times, they also tell the purchaser to just provide the product review and they'll post it.[19]

Those faux reviews aren't just inconvenient. If left unchecked, they represent a significant threat to Amazon's business because customer reviews are downright essential today. In December 2015, search engine optimization outfit BrightLocal found that 88 percent of consumers trust online reviews as much as personal recommendations. Nearly 40 percent "regularly" read online product reviews and only 12 percent did not.†

COMPANIES LEFT BEHIND

Of course, not every company and industry has benefited from the technology and data revolutions. To borrow a line from *Breaking Bad*, I want to tread lightly here. I am certainly not looking to make enemies.

---

*See *60 Minutes*' fascinating segment on how fake news spreads at http://cbsn .ws/2o75MB0.

†Read the whole study at http://bit.ly/2dDB2o8.

It's fair to say, though, that the publishing industry as a whole arrived late to the data and analytics party. Compared to Amazon, traditional publishers and large bookstores such as Barnes & Noble have struggled. (Borders filed for Chapter 11 bankruptcy in February 2011.) In large part, these firms haven't maintained direct relationships with their customers. They often don't know who buys their books. At least they are not alone.

Many brick-and-mortar retailers also have suffered from their inability to tailor offerings to potential customers who walk through their doors. This is why there's so much industry excitement around location-based technologies such as Apple's iBeacon. (Think of the infamous commercials in *Minority Report*.) Equipped with real-time data, Target, Home Depot, Macy's, and other big-box retailers may represent more than mere showrooms for Amazon, a company that largely avoids the considerable expenses associated with maintaining physical stores.

THE GROWTH OF ANALYTICS PROGRAMS

Do you still doubt that analytics matter more than ever? I hope that this chapter has convinced you. In case you're still on the fence, consider the following.

Higher education needs to evolve to stay relevant, especially in an era of massive open online courses, staggering levels of college debt, and Thiel Fellows.* More U.S. colleges and universities than ever are offering formal programs in analytics and data science.[20] I am fortunate enough to teach at one of the best ones. I would be mystified if this trend abates anytime soon. Beyond accredited academic programs, there are plenty of informal ways to increase your knowledge in the field. Coursera, Udemy, and other online learning companies have followed suit with individual courses and programs, many of which cost nothing.

---

* Controversial billionaire Peter Thiel gives 20 smart young cookies $100,000 each year to start their own companies and forgo college.

CHAPTER REVIEW AND DISCUSSION QUESTIONS

- What do you think of Steve Jobs's stance regarding the *New York Times*?
- What types of things could Apple do with this type of customer information? What types of apps could it recommend?
- What types of data does Uber capture? How can it analyze that data in ways that traditional taxi and transportation companies cannot?
  - What types of experiments can Uber run?
  - How else would you use this data?
  - How could you change the Uber app to collect even more information?
- Now imagine that you are Airbnb CEO Brian Chesky. What kinds of questions could you ask and answer of your company's data?
- How would you use that information?
- Could bookstores and traditional publishers have embraced new technologies and data sources more quickly? What specifically could each have done?
- Do you think that any of these moves ultimately would have made a difference, or are disruption and marginalization inevitable?

NEXT

This chapter establishes today's tech-, data-, and analytics-heavy business context. Now it's time to take a step back. Just what do *data* and *analytics* mean, anyway?

The next chapter answers this key question.

NOTES

1. Justin Fox, "How to Succeed in Business by Bundling—and Unbundling," *Harvard Business Review*, June 24, 2014, http://tinyurl.com/h8ld3eb.
2. Daniel Nations, "How Many iPads Have Been Sold?," March 15, 2017, http://tinyurl.com/z93lpml.
3. Charles Babcock, "Amazon: The Self-Fueling, Perpetual Motion Machine," *InformationWeek*, January 9, 2017, http://ubm.io/2j4NkJF.
4. Roger Clarke, "Information Wants to Be Free . . . ," August 28, 2001, http://bit.ly/12V0o8m.

5. Matthew Panzarino, "Apple's Tim Cook Delivers Blistering Speech on Encryption, Privacy," *TechCrunch*, June 2, 2015, http://tcrn.ch/2nSK2YI.

6. Peter Sayer, "Apple, Microsoft Wield Privacy as Marketing Tool," *Computerworld*, September 29, 2015, http://tinyurl.com/z7ckvyc.

7. Lisa Morgan, "12 Ways to Cultivate a Data-Savvy Workforce," *InformationWeek*, July 7, 2016, http://ubm.io/29pbiJX.

8. Will Oremus, "Tech Companies Are Dominating the Stock Market as Never Before," *Moneybox*, July 29, 2016, http://tinyurl.com/gkpsdtk.

9. Alexei Oreskovic, "Amazon Isn't Just Growing Revenue Anymore—It's Growing Profits," *Business Insider*, April 28, 2016, http://tinyurl.com/z3d42j2.

10. Peter Kafka, "Sold! (Finally) Facebook Takes Atlas from Microsoft, So It Can Get Serious about Ads," *All Things*, February 28, 2013, http://tinyurl.com/d6htpbm.

11. Anthony Ha, "Facebook Is Making Its Cross-Device Atlas Data Available to More Advertisers," *TechCrunch*, March 7, 2017, https://techcrunch.com/2017/03/07/facebook-advanced-measurement.

12. Greg Bensinger, "Amazon Wants to Ship Your Package Before You Buy It," *Wall Street Journal*, January 17, 2014, http://on.wsj.com/1h7X1m8.

13. Jessica Rawden, "The Insane Amount of Money Netflix Will Spend on Content in 2016," *CinemaBlend*, March 1, 2016, http://tinyurl.com/h9jdytt.

14. Cristina Alesci and Kate Trafecante, "Uber Prices Surge on New Year's Eve," CNN, January 2, 2015, http://tinyurl.com/cnnuber6.

15. Lisa Qian, "How Well Does NPS Predict Rebooking?," Airbnb Engineering & Data Science, December 10, 2016, http://nerds.airbnb.com/nps-rebooking.

16. Dan Frommer, "Chart of the Day: The BlackBerry's Fall to 0.0 Percent Market Share," *Recode*, February 26, 2017, http://tinyurl.com/jcbxfwu.

17. Marco della Cava, "Lyft Looks to Raise $500M as Uber Stumbles," *USA Today*, March 2, 2017, http://usat.ly/2mDwLWM.

18. Joshua Gillin, "How Pizzagate Went from Fake News to a Real Problem for a D.C. Business," *Politifact*, December 5, 2016, http://bit.ly/2gZE862.

19. Sarah Perez, "Amazon Files Suit against Individuals Offering Fake Product Reviews on Fiverr.com," *TechCrunch*, October 16, 2015, http://tcrn.ch/2lHlOnR.

20. J. Maureen Henderson, "Are Degrees in Big Data a Fad or a Fast Track to Career Success?," *Forbes*, July 30, 2013, http://tinyurl.com/hhrqc7d.

CHAPTER 2

The Fundamentals of Contemporary Data

A Primer on What It Is, Why It Matters, and How to Get It

We are drowning in information and starving for knowledge.

—Rutherford D. Rogers

When you refer to a *car*, most people know what you mean. Sure, depending on where you live, you may call it an *automobile, voiture,* or *coche*. That's not to say, though, that all cars are created equal. They are not. Souped-up Porsches and Lamborghinis run hundreds of thousands of dollars, while used Pintos cost mere hundreds. Some cars run only on diesel fuel, and an increasing number require no fuel at all—and then there are the hybrids. More distinctions are on their way. Soon some cars will drive themselves. Others already do—sometimes. Tesla currently sports a semiautonomous model, the Model S.

TYPES OF DATA

But does the same hold true for *data*? Does everyone immediately know what you mean when you use the term?

For those looking to really apply analytics, the umbrella term *data* represents an ultimately unfulfilling starting point. The *type* of data at your disposal governs much of what you can do with it and how you need to do it. Against that backdrop, when we talk about data, we're really referring to four different kinds:

1. Structured
2. Semistructured
3. Unstructured
4. Metadata

Let's briefly explore each.

Structured

When laypersons and even many professionals think of data, they usually picture Microsoft Excel. Perhaps they conjure up lists of sales, leads, employees, paychecks, and transactions. This type of data lends itself to easy calculations. Realtors who want to know the number and average price of their sales by month usually don't need much help.

Structured data is critical to just about every enterprise—large and small. Try paying your employees, running a profit-and-loss (P&L) statement, or assessing the health of your business without structured data. Table 2.1 provides an example.

Table 2.1 Sample of Structured Data from Fictional Employee Table*

Employee	First Name	Last Name	Salary
7777	Mark	Kelly	100,000
7778	Steve	Hogarth	110,000
7779	Pete	Trawavas	99,000
7780	Steven	Rothery	103,455
7781	Ian	Mosley	105,000

Source: Phil Simon.

*The astute reader will recognize these names and how underpaid these men are in this example.

Still, structured data is not the only game in town. In fact, it represents only about 10 percent of the data available.[1]

Semistructured

Go to your e-mail inbox now. I'll wait. Really. What do you see?

Odds are that you see thousands of Amazon order confirmations, invitations, Groupon offers, and even a few spam messages. You may have never thought of them as proper *data*, but they are. They are just a different type of data than that which you find in spreadsheets.

E-mail is the classic example of semistructured data. Elements of each message are structured: Each message's date, time sent, whether the sender marked it as *urgent*, and the sender's e-mail address are highly organized. As such, they lend themselves to quick calculations. For instance, it is very easy to count the number of messages that you received from your boss last Monday morning.

There's a great deal of information in each message, though, that is anything but structured. The content of the e-mail may range from a few words to several thousand. The message may contain links to other websites. Messages often contain attachments in the form of Microsoft Office documents, PDFs, pictures, and MP3 files. Using traditional methods, it is far more difficult to answer basic questions about unstructured data, such as:

- How many of your boss's Monday-morning e-mails contained vital information?
- How many of them really weren't that important after all?*

Unstructured

You may not have heard of the term *unstructured data*, but you interact with it on a regular basis:

- Each Netflix and YouTube video you watch
- Every status update you post on social networks such as Facebook, LinkedIn, and Twitter
- Ditto for photos you take and share with others
- Any article, blog post, or Yelp review you read
- Even the games you play

If you haven't already guessed: These things don't play nicely with spreadsheets and relational databases. Try uploading photos in Google Sheets and performing a simple sort. Try calculating simple subtotals on user videos in Microsoft Excel or a relational database. While remarkably useful, these applications weren't built to handle these unwieldy data types.

Fortunately, you're in luck. Techniques for parsing and *understanding* unstructured data have exploded in recent years—along with the tools supporting them. Today, they include the following:

- Sentiment analysis
- Text mining
- Natural language programming, artificial intelligence, and machine learning
- High-performance computing

---

* Interestingly, increasingly sophisticated tools are unearthing trends in massive datasets of e-mails. See http://bit.ly/2n7jl1D.

At a high level, these techniques and their associate tools help find signals in noisy unstructured data. For instance, you could discern relationships among Yelp reviews and specific words.*

Metadata

One of the easiest ways to understand unstructured data is to look at the metadata associated with it. For example, consider Twitter, the beleaguered social network that somehow remains relevant despite its alarming executive turnover and toxic corporate culture. (For more on this, see "ESP at Twitter" later in this chapter.) The company that popularized those iconic 140 characters tracks a great deal more than most people realize.

As Paul Ford wrote for *Bloomberg*, "In fact, those 140 characters are less than 10 percent of all the data you'll find in a tweet object."[2] As of November 2013, its 31 publicly documented data fields included tweet location, device, latitude, and longitude. But it doesn't stop there. Twitter can tell whether each tweet potentially raises copyright flags. Twitter also knows whether certain countries would censor it and whether it contains potentially sensitive information, and the like.

Outed by Metadata

Alicia Keys found out the hard way that those digital bread crumbs you leave can haunt you. In January 2013, beleaguered smartphone maker BlackBerry—formerly Research in Motion—had hired Keys as its "global creative director." Perhaps she could infuse some energy into the moribund company and its sullied brand.

Shortly after accepting the position at a reported $1 million salary, the pop singer was fired by BlackBerry for a tweet.[3] No, she didn't slam her employer, nor did she praise the competition—at least not directly. She sent out an inspirational tweet on February 11, 2013, at 9:10 a.m. with the words "Started from the bottom now were [*sic*]

---

*For a detailed example, see http://varianceexplained.org/r/yelp-sentiment.

here!" Automatically attached to the tweet without her knowledge were the words "via Twitter for iPhone."

Lest you think Keys's story is an isolated occurrence, think again. As former FedEx CEO Frederick W. Smith once said, "The information about the package is as important as the package itself."

The Power of Boring

We all know that security matters—or at least we should. For instance, leaked quarterly earnings can spell disaster for investors who lack that information. Job postings on ostensibly secret projects can shed light into a company's future products and services. And then there are the routine, high-profile, and increasingly dangerous hacks.

None of this should surprise you, but here's something that might: even boring metadata such as check sequence numbers might reveal a heck of a lot more than you would think.

My friend, noted author and security guru Mike Schrenk, illustrates how easily this can happen. In one of our conversations, he described to me one of his retail side businesses. He receives monthly affiliate payments from a company that we'll call Golden Moth Chemical (GMC) here.* His affiliate rate is 10 percent.

GMC sends its affiliates physical checks, each of which contains valuable pieces of—you guessed it—metadata such as check data and number. Schrenk knew that check amounts varied by month, but the numbers seemed to be sequential and predictable. Table 2.2 shows a simple example of what he described with dummy data.

Table 2.2 Affiliate Payments from GMC

Check Date	Check Number	Check Amount
1/31/13	1234	$28.12
2/28/13	1254	$30.07
3/31/13	1275	$31.04

Source: Phil Simon.

---

* Yes, it's another *Breaking Bad* reference.

As shown in Table 2.2, Schrenk received an average monthly check of about $30 from GMC. However, the sequence of check numbers gave him an incredibly valuable and unexpected insight into GMC's financial situation: The company appeared to cut only about 20 checks per month. Let's say that Schrenk's side business accurately represented GMC's other customers. Equipped with this information, Schrenk deduced that the company was generating roughly $562 in monthly commissions. At a 10 percent commission rate, this meant that GMC's annual sales totaled approximately $60,000.

All from a little metadata.

Is this model foolproof? Of course not, and the only way to truly verify this information is to look at GMC's books. As Schrenk freely admitted, for all he knew, GMC paid different rates to larger or smaller vendors. Still, it's safe to say that GMC management probably did not know that it potentially tipped its hand on the health of its finances via something as prosaic as check numbers.

GMC's management is hardly alone in ignoring digital bread crumbs and metadata. I certainly can't compile a list of everything that an organization ought to lock down, but it's evident that even seemingly useless information can be very useful under the right circumstances.

PRISM

Edward Snowden leaked word of the U.S. government's PRISM program in June 2013. As Glenn Greenwald recounts in his excellent book *No Place to Hide*, the scandal took administration officials and politicians by surprise. Reporters scurried to gather details on what may have been the largest spying program in world history. In the words of White House spokesman Josh Earnest, "The information acquired does not include *the content* of any communications."* [Emphasis added.] Put differently, the government was not looking at specific phone calls and e-mails, just its metadata. No big deal, right?

---

* See http://tinyurl.com/j9yjs9q.

Not so fast. Metadata reveals much more than most of us realize. As Alex Hern wrote for *The Guardian*:

> Researchers there successfully identified a cannabis cultivator, multiple sclerosis sufferer and a visitor to an abortion clinic using nothing more than the timing and destination of their phone calls.[4]

Think about it. A woman who calls a family-planning service three times in a week isn't ordering a pizza. It's not a wrong number.

GETTING THE DATA

I'll bet that at some point in your career you'll work on a project that qualifies as *Agile analytics*. Perhaps your company keeps its internal systems in impeccable shape. As a result, you receive a pristine dataset with every field that you could conceivably want. All of the metadata is there as well, so, if you have any questions, you can easily see who did what when.

I strongly suspect, though, that things won't go nearly this smoothly for any large analytics endeavor. Even if they do, I'd argue that you're missing out.

To elaborate, an enterprise may already possess a great deal of data on its customers, users, employees, and partners. Invariably, there's even more valuable data outside of its walls. (Authors have written entire books about open data and linked data.) Analytics increasingly requires facility with new extraction tools, software applications, and data-exchange formats.

This is what separates a traditional statistician from a proper data scientist: the latter knows how to go out and get the data. Figure 2.1 shows an accurate tweet on the matter.

You may not consider yourself a *data scientist*, but analytics today requires more than just interpreting data. It necessitates the ability to generate and gather data as well. Those are the subjects of the remainder of this chapter.

Data Scientist (n.): Person who is better at statistics than any software engineer and better at software engineering than any statistician.

RETWEETS	LIKES	
1,577	**1,208**	

9:55 AM - 3 May 2012

↩ 52   ↻ 1.6K   ♥ 1.2K

Figure 2.1 Tweet about Data Scientists
Source: @josh_wills, Twitter, May 3, 2012.

Generating Data

Today, there are scores of ways to generate your own data. That's not to say, though, that all data-generation efforts are equal. They're not. As the following example illustrates, the most intelligent way involves converting semistructured or unstructured data into a more structured format.

Surveys and Polls

Soon after signing the contract to write this book, I mocked up some cover designs via the design site Canva. I then wrote a post on my website that included those mock-ups. I asked people to vote on their preferences.* To spark even more interest, feedback, and data, I did two things. First, I updated my public Facebook status with a link to that post. Second, I shared the post in a private Facebook group of experienced and successful writers called Write and Rant (see Figure 2.2).

---

* See the post at http://tinyurl.com/zdmc6xg.

Figure 2.2 Write and Rant Facebook Post
Source: Facebook post on March 2, 2017.

There was a method to my madness. Sure, individual responses provided valuable third-party input from friends, and in the case of the Facebook group, successful peers. At the same time, though, individual comments *by themselves* do not represent the best way for me to understand which one of my cover options resonated most strongly with my friends and potential book buyers. For this very reason, I encouraged those with opinions to vote in the poll that I created via Google Forms.

This is important. I don't "own" the comments in the Write and Rant thread. The group's admin could easily have deleted my post, eliminating my valuable feedback in the process. In other words, by driving traffic to the poll on my site, I was able to easily collect user votes and interpret their results. Figure 2.3 shows voters' initial reactions.

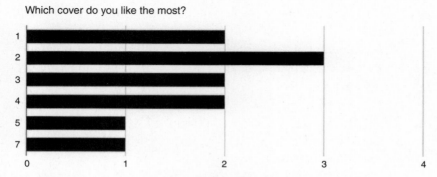

Figure 2.3 Initial Results of Cover Poll for *Analytics: The Agile Way* Cover Vote
Source: Data generated via Google Forms. Figure from Phil Simon.

No single one-question poll can capture every conceivable opinion on even a simple question. My cover mock-up poll is no exception. The lesson here is that some data-collection methods are superior to others. A simple Facebook, Twitter, or SurveyMonkey poll lends itself to the simple tabulation of responses; you need not manually parse through text-laden replies to determine its results.

Asking others to provide data via surveys, polls, and social media is hardly the only way to generate your own data these days. Consider two other powerful, easy, and increasingly popular ways to easily generate a boatload of valuable data.

Web Scraping

Despite the vast and ever-increasing amount of data on the Web, much of it doesn't lend itself to meaningful analysis—at least with traditional programs. This is doubly true if you limit yourself to stalwarts such as Microsoft Excel and even relational databases. (Behind the scenes, much of that data exists in a much more structured format typically called the *back end*.) Forget Google search results or an Amazon product page. Try copying and pasting the contents of even a simple web page into most mainstream productivity applications and you'll see what I mean. Still, if a web page contains a decent amount of data that you would like to gather in a systematic way, you should not just manually input values. More than ever, you have options for capturing it in a structured manner. User-friendly web scrapers such as import.io, Mozenda, IFTTT,* and others allow anyone with reasonable computer skills to act as an amateur data scientist.

As the following example illustrates, you need not be a programmer or hacker to retrieve data from popular websites and conduct more traditional data analyses.

Among my longtime clients is SAS, the analytics company. Over the years, I have written hundreds of posts on *The Data Roundtable,*[†] one of the company's blogs. The site runs on WordPress, the most

---

* To be fair, IFTTT lets you do quite a bit more than scrape data.
[†] Read as many as you like here: http://blogs.sas.com/content/author/philsimon.

popular content-management system in the world. (More than one-quarter of all sites use WordPress.) Figure 2.4 presents the front page of the blog as of December 16, 2016.

Figure 2.4 *Data Roundtable* Front Page as of December 16, 2016
Source: SAS/Phil Simon.

I was curious about how many page views my blog post generated compared to my peers'. Were my posts more or less popular than those of the site's other bloggers?

To be sure, the front page and subsequent pages contain plenty of data relevant to my query. Still, that data was not in a form that let me easily answer my question. Within five minutes, via import.io, I was able to produce a structured list of 600 of the site's most recent posts along with author name, post data, number of page views, and the like. Figure 2.5 shows the results of my scraping efforts.

	author_name	date	title	page_views
1	Jim Harris	February 29, 2016	How big of a deal is big data quality?	2463
2	Dylan Jones	February 23, 2016	Scaling a vision for data quality	2966
3	Phil Simon	February 18, 2016	Who's in charge of data quality?	2210

Figure 2.5 Results of Web Scraping via import.io
Source: import.io/Phil Simon.

With very little time and effort, I was able to pull unstructured data. Five minutes later, I derived insights into the popularity of my own posts and plenty of other things. What's more, a few mouse clicks later, I was creating my own data visualizations in Google Sheets (see Figure 2.6).

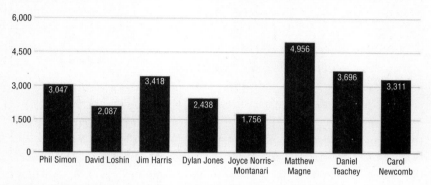

Figure 2.6 Page Views by Author on *Data Roundtable*
Source: Data generated from Data Roundtable, *scraped via import.io, and analyzed with Google Sheets. Figure from Phil Simon.*

To be fair, import.io does not always yield comprehensive and perfectly formatted results. While it is certainly user-friendly, it is not the most powerful scraper out there. By some estimates, roughly 90 percent of all data on the Web is of the unstructured variety, and much of it doesn't play nicely with scrapers. What's more, no scraper will work with every website. For instance, Facebook bans the practice of scraping and will boot users who violate this policy from the site.*

Limitations aside, though, import.io was perfect for my simple needs. It saves its users a great deal of time. I demonstrate it to my students each semester.

❷ TIP

More technically inclined folks can play with a variety of parsing alternatives. In Python, for instance, consider Beautiful Soup† or Scrapy,‡ a fast and powerful web-crawling framework.

---

* See http://bit.ly/2nxzRKo.
† Learn more at http://bit.ly/2mWOS9P.
‡ Check it out at http://scrapy.org.

Tapping into APIs

Whether you know it or not, if you use a smartphone app or surf the Web these days, you're benefiting from application program interfaces (APIs). At a high level, APIs specify how disparate software components should interact with one another. Think of them as essential building blocks that allow for easier software development and, more important, linking together related services. It's no overstatement to say that many apps wouldn't exist today without APIs—at least in their current form. Case in point: import.io (mentioned in the previous section).

APIs allow developers to do more than build games. They let techies retrieve valuable pieces of data and do interesting things with them. For instance, let's say that you wanted to build an application that notifies companies when others have left reviews for their products on Amazon. That is, for any given Amazon Standard Identification Number (ASIN),* you want to receive a push alert.

Amazon makes developing these types of applications easier than ever. As I wrote in *The Age of the Platform* in 2011, APIs are taking off—a trend that has only intensified in the past six years. Many companies today have built their own APIs or even *sets* of APIs, although not all APIs are public. We're seeing the rise of private APIs.†

Format Matters

Odds are that at some point you have worked with a comma-separated value (CSV) file, perhaps in Microsoft Excel or Access or even a text editor. For a long time, this format was the gold standard in data circles. Figure 2.7 shows an example of a very simple CSV.

```
firstName,lastName
Emilio,Koyama
Skyler,White
Hank,Schrader
```

Figure 2.7 Simple CSV Example
Source: Phil Simon.

---

* From Amazon's API documentation, an ASIN is "a positive integer distributed by Amazon that uniquely identifies an item." For more, see http://amzn.to/2m9VuCZ.
† See http://bit.ly/2mQtMbz.

No longer does the CSV format represent the only—or often the best—way to store and transmit data, especially over the Web and within apps. The past 10 years have seen the growth of two other lightweight data-interchange formats particularly suited for web services and APIs: JavaScript Object Notation (JSON) and eXtensible Markup Language (XML). Although you can use either format to receive data from web servers, there are some significant differences between the two.

JSON is an open-standard format. It uses human-readable (read: self-describing) text to transmit data objects consisting of attribute-value pairs.* Figure 2.8 shows the same data in JSON format.

```
{"employees":[
    { "firstName":"Emilio", "lastName":"Koyama" },
    { "firstName":"Skyler", "lastName":"White" },
    { "firstName":"Hank", "lastName":"Schrader" }
]}
```

Figure 2.8 Simple JSON Example

Source: Phil Simon.

XML is a text format derived from Standard Generalized Markup Language, or SGML. It is text-based and position-independent.† Its fans cite its openness and interoperability as benefits. Figure 2.9 shows the same data from the previous examples in XML format.

```
<employees>
    <employee>
        <firstName>Emilio</firstName> <lastName>Koyama</lastName>
    </employee>
    <employee>
        <firstName>Skyler</firstName> <lastName>White</lastName>
    </employee>
    <employee>
        <firstName>Hank</firstName> <lastName>Schrader</lastName>
    </employee>
</employees>
```

Figure 2.9 Simple XML Example

Source: Phil Simon.

---

*Think of a table containing columns that designate different attributes. If you want to say it in a fancier way, it's a basic knowledge-representation framework.

†This means that it executes properly regardless of its absolute address, whether it's on line number 1 or line number 1,000.

For several reasons, JSON is the more popular protocol of the two these days. (Google Trends confirms what I have suspected for some time now.*) First, JSON tends to transmit faster than XML because the former stores and transfers less data. JSON can do this because it employs a hierarchical model—that is, it organizes data into a tree-like structure. This makes JSON both more compact, simpler, and arguably more readable than XML. (Some have called it the "fat-free alternative to XML.") By using a standard JavaScript function [JSON.parse()], a coder can parse the data and it immediately becomes a JavaScript object—JavaScript loves objects.

Conceptually, XML works the same as JSON. Still, many developers complain that the former is too verbose compared to the latter. XML also doesn't match the data model of most mainstream programming languages. Next, parsing it requires an XML parser, something that irritates many programmers.[†] As someone put it in a thread on the popular site HackerNews, "XML is a markup language. It's for documents. Don't use it for data."[‡]

❓**TIP**

Don't be afraid to play around with different data-exchange formats. The CSV is no longer the only game in town. Depending on your needs, the others might suit your project or app better.

Buying Data

By some accounts, data brokering is a $200 billion annual industry[5] largely exempt from government regulation, something unlikely to change in the current U.S. political climate. I'm willing to bet that you can't name a single data broker—and that's exactly how the industry

---

* See https://trends.google.com/trends/explore?q=json,xml.
[†] For more on the limitations of XML, see http://bit.ly/2mnfiRW.
[‡] See http://bit.ly/2m0u8dE.

likes it. In fact, data brokers generally eschew the term altogether. For instance, Acxiom brands itself as "a marketing technology and services company." That sounds fairly benign, and its executives certainly prefer it to the sinister term *data broker*. For its part, Slice Intelligence provides critical "competitive intelligence" in the form of data, and analytics to Uber, furthering the car-sharing company's attempts to crush its rivals.[6]

DATA IN MOTION

Historically, most analytics involved data that enterprises had captured and stored in a proper database or data warehouse. That is, the data was "at rest." Sure, there were exceptions to this rule, but they were limited to relatively specialized fields. Capital markets, pharmaceutical research, and energy production come to mind. Thanks to the rise of social media, smartphones, cheap sensors, and the Internet of Things (discussed in Chapter 1), this is changing.

Over the past decade, we've seen a rise in *streaming data* or *data in motion*. Put simply, this means millions of transactions *constantly* emanating from equipment, devices, apps, and APIs. Technologies discussed earlier in this chapter such as relational database management systems weren't designed to handle—much less interpret—data of this quantity and speed.

As a result, we've seen the development of new sets of tools under the umbrellas of *event-stream processing* (ESP) or *complex event processing* (CEP). At a high level, they do the following two things:

1. Aggregate data from multiple sources.
2. Infer nonobvious events or patterns from these sources.

Often used interchangeably, ESP and CEP try to identify meaningful events from never-ending data streams. Once the technologies have isolated opportunities and threats, users and downstream systems can quickly respond to them. (The next chapter will return to ESP and CEP within the context of analytics.)

ESP AT TWITTER

In the past, I've been critical of Twitter on several fronts. First and foremost, its core "product"* fails the "Mom test." Although your mother probably understands Facebook, the same is unlikely true about Twitter and its dizzying user interface. Next, Twitter's communication strategy is downright confusing.† Its chaotic culture has led to a comical and interminable executive merry-go-round not unlike that of Spinal Tap drummers. Nick Bilton's excellent book *Hatching Twitter* delves into its founders' Machiavellian tendencies.

On a different level, its management has persistently and stubbornly refused to combat trolling and bullying. Only recently has it started making substantive changes in its product.

Twitter remains fascinating, though: I'm hard-pressed to think of a company that has succeeded so much in spite of itself.

Its significant faults aside, Twitter remains an important communication and news medium—as long as it avoids the fail whale. To this end, the company has consistently upgraded its infrastructure as it has grown. On the average day, Twitter hosts around 500 million tweets.‡ If you think that Twitter can store—much less interpret—that much information using CSV files and a relational database such as Oracle, then you're sorely mistaken.

In June 2015, the company announced the launch of its new real-time streaming system Heron.[7] (If you want to dive into its technical details, read the link in the endnote.) Its API also streams messages encoded in JSON. (See "Format Matters" earlier in this chapter.)

---

*I qualify this term because one typically has to spend money on a proper product.

† See http://bit.ly/2nsQtlj.

‡ For more interesting Twitter facts, see www.internetlivestats.com/twitter-statistics.

 TIP

As Twitter manifests, making sense out of streaming data usually means quite a bit more than plugging new cables into existing outlets. You will probably require entirely new electronics and circuitry if you want the power to stay on.

CHAPTER REVIEW AND DISCUSSION QUESTIONS

- The term *Big Data* consists of four more specific types of data. What are they? Provide an example of each.
- Can you think of a way to turn an unstructured dataset into a more structured one?
- What tools would you use to do this?
- Are there any limitations to what you're capturing?
- We know that employees shouldn't indiscriminately share confidential data with competitors and the public at large. Think back to the GMC example. What kinds of information are companies inadvertently letting web sleuths know?

NEXT

This chapter covered today's complex and expansive data landscape. In the next, we'll review the practice of *analytics*. Chapter 3 provides an overview of that catchall term.

NOTES

1. Mark Barrenechea, "Big Data: Big Hype?," *Forbes*, February 4, 2013, http://tinyurl.com/gu6sn4c.
2. Paul Ford, "The Hidden Technology That Makes Twitter Huge," *Bloomberg*, November 7, 2013, http://tinyurl.com/gnguj96.
3. "Alicia Keys Loses Creative Director Gig at BlackBerry," CNBC, January 2, 2014, http://tinyurl.com/keys-meta.
4. Alex Hern, "Phone Call Metadata Does Betray Sensitive Details about Your Life—Study," *The Guardian*, March 13, 2014, http://tinyurl.com/j6j4rx4.
5. Yasha Levine, "Surveillance Valley Scammers! Why Hack Our Data When You Can Just Buy It?," Pando, January 8, 2014, http://bit.ly/2lZRUGz.
6. Mike Isaac, "Uber's C.E.O. Plays with Fire," *New York Times*, April 23, 2017, http://nyti.ms/2oidfkx.
7. Karthik Ramasamy, "Flying Faster with Twitter Heron," Twitter, June 2, 2015, http://bit.ly/1RHLgzz.

CHAPTER 3

The Fundamentals of Analytics

Peeling Back the Onion

Life must be lived forwards but can only be understood backwards.

—Søren Kierkegaard

Y ou'll get no argument from me about the power of analytics. I've seen it firsthand, and I wouldn't have written this book if I didn't grasp its potential to make better decisions. As is often the case today, though, there's no shortage of hype around it. As I wrote in *Message Not Received,* far too many software vendors, consulting firms, industry experts, and talking heads often exacerbate matters with buzzwords, forced "backronyms," and opaque models that confuse far more than they convey.

This brief chapter shines a spotlight on the different types of analytics.

DEFINING ANALYTICS

At a high level, I like to think of *analytics* as the process of using raw data to derive valuable insights and increase understanding of a topic. By analyzing historical and current events, you can identify potential trends. Analytics allows individuals, groups, and even entire organizations to make optimal—or at least better-informed— decisions.

More than ever, these decisions run the gamut. Today, they involve making money, identifying errors, and mitigating risk, as well as reducing costs, customer churn, or employee turnover. Analytics are useful irrespective of company size and in just about every industry. Many nonprofits use analytics, as does just about every major sports franchise these days.

Analytics go beyond simple statistics. Let's say that an organization's employee turnover rate is 5 percent or that Clyde Drexler averaged 20.4 points per game during his NBA career. That's great, but unfortunately neither qualifies as *analytics*.

Finally, despite their considerable advantages, analytics is not a panacea. As I'll discuss later in this chapter, it does not guarantee successful outcomes. (Chapter 13 will broach other analytics-related myths and impediments.) All else being equal, though, organizations that effective use analytics will do better than their analytically challenged brethren. As Charles Babbage so eloquently said, "Errors using inadequate data are much less than those using no data at all."

Reporting ≠ Analytics

The term *analytics* has replaced *key performance indicators* in the contemporary business vernacular. Figure 3.1 shows how Google

Trends has ranked the relative popularity of these two terms over the past decade.

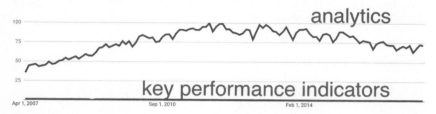

Figure 3.1 Google Trends: Analytics versus Key Performance Indicators (March 7, 2007, to March 7, 2017)
Source: Data from Google Trends. Figure from Phil Simon.

Analytics and *key performance indicators* may refer to the same general concept, but you should not lump all data-related terms together. Although plenty of people speak in jargon-laden terms, precision in language counts. To this end, it's important to distinguish between *analytics* and *reporting*.

Let me be unequivocally clear: These are not synonyms. Reporting is not the same as analytics, and I am not the only one who feels this way. In *Taming the Big Data Tidal Wave*, Bill Franks differentiates between the two, as shown in Table 3.1.

Table 3.1 Reporting versus Analytics

Reporting	Analysis
Provides data	Provides answers
Provides what is asked for	Provides what is needed
Is typically standardized	Is typically customized
Does not involve a person	Involves a person
Is fairly inflexible	Is extremely flexible

Source: Modified from Taming the Big Data Tidal Wave by Bill Franks.

A Disclaimer

Before continuing, note that Table 3.1 represents a bit of a false dichotomy. It's tempting to conclude that analytics are innately powerful, and reporting is inherently limited. While this is doubtless true in many instances, I'd stop short of saying this is a universal truth. I have seen good, simple reports and incomplete and misleading analytics. Beyond that, some reports remain downright essential to running a business* and complying with government regulations.

The Limitations of Traditional Reporting

In my consulting career, I spent a great deal of time creating reports for my clients. These have included:

- Writing several thousand Crystal Reports
- Creating more Microsoft Access databases, SQL statements, and ad hoc queries than I could count
- Building many, many dashboards

Some of these reports didn't just qualify as *complicated*. (A few, in particular, were real doozies.) They would detail what, where, and when business events happened. Still, not that many reports or dashboards really explained *why* something was happening or had already happened. In other words, these reports usually didn't qualify as proper *analytics*. Ideally, analytics explains *why* something occurred.

 TIP

The best analytics suggest a corrective and measurable course of action.

For instance, how many customers visited your company's website and never made a purchase? Let's say that number is 60 percent. That's great, but *why* did "the leavers"† not make a purchase? Potential answers include:

- The product's price was too high.
- The site's navigation was confusing.

---

*Tried-and-true cash flow statements and trial balances fall under this umbrella.
†Yes, this is a Marillion reference.

- They became distracted while completing the purchase.
- The site declined customers' credit cards.
- Their computers crashed or their smartphones died.
- A combination of a few different things occurred.

I could go on, but you get my drift. A simple standard report or statistic isn't entirely unhelpful, but all too often it begs the question: Why? Standard reports often don't help in this regard.

More than ever, organizations of all sizes can theoretically explain more of the unknown, and dare I say, even potentially predict a few things. To truly realize the value of data—be it Big, small, whatever—people need to rid themselves of the notion that standard reports equate to meaningful analytics, let alone true data discovery.

TYPES OF ANALYTICS

Much like *data* (see "Types of Data" in Chapter 2), *analytics* is a catch-all term. While there's hardly unanimity among the cognoscenti, analytics generally falls into three buckets: descriptive, predictive, and prescriptive.

Descriptive Analytics

Put simply, descriptive analytics summarizes or describes what is happening now or what has happened. That is, it can focus on the present or can look backward. When doing the latter, it attempts to explain and gain new insights from historical events.

Consider for a moment Lleyton Hewitt, the Australian men's tennis player who held the number-one ranking before Roger Federer's ascension. At 5'11" and 170 pounds, Hewitt was not physically imposing. What he lacked in stature, though, he more than made up for with his legendary intensity and impeccable movement on the court.

Hewitt routinely raised his game against opponents ranked in the top 10. As Table 3.2 illustrates, this was particularly true during the 2001 season:[1]

Table 3.2 Lleyton Hewitt's 2001 Performance versus Top 50 and Top 10 Players

Hewitt's 2001 Season	Vs. Top 50	Vs. Top 10
Return rating	160.2 (8th)	178.8 (1st)
Return games won	30.7% (5th)	37% (1st)
First-serve return points won	33.4% (9th)	35% (1st)
Break points converted	43.4% (7th)	51.4% (1st)
Tie-breaks won	58.3% (16th)	100% (T-1st)
Second-serve return points won	53.7% (9th)	55.4% (3rd)

Source: Data from ATP World Tour. Table from Phil Simon.

No one can credibly call Hewitt the greatest of all time, but perhaps no one played better than he did against the game's best players. (As the data shows, he performed better against elite players than he did against merely good ones, especially in 2001.)

Predictive Analytics

Many people misunderstand this class of analytics. Perhaps this is because *predictive analytics* is a relatively new term that seems to have replaced *modeling* and *forecasting* in the business vernacular.

Irrespective of moniker, predictive analytics ironically can't *really* predict anything. Even analytics pioneer Billy Beane's newfangled statistics hardly guaranteed success. (See "The *Moneyball* Effect" in Chapter 1.) In the words of Dr. Michael Wu, chief scientist of San Francisco–based Lithium Technologies:

> The purpose of predictive analytics is not to tell you what will happen in the future. It cannot do that. In fact, no analytics can do that. Predictive analytics can only forecast what might happen in the future because *all predictive analytics are probabilistic in nature.*[2] [Emphasis added.]

This last point is crucial. As Nassim Taleb described in *The Black Swan: The Impact of the Highly Improbable*, even extremely rare occurrences (aka *black swans*) do happen over a sufficiently long period of time. The 2016 U.S. presidential election sadly proved the following rule: Never confuse low-probability events with zero-probability events.

GOOD CASINO BETS

In a casino, only a fool believes that all bets are created equal. There are good bets and bad ones.

For instance, in blackjack, players can win in one of two ways: by drawing cards and coming closer to 21 without exceeding that number (*busting* in gambling parlance) or by waiting for the dealer to bust. Dealers have to hit if their cards total 16 or lower. Unfortunately for you, only one of the dealer's cards is visible.

You sit down at the last seat at table (on the dealer's right) and plunk down $20. You are not counting cards, and you don't want to earn the enmity of the experienced players at the table. You are holding a jack and a seven (17 total). The dealer's "up card" is a six. Do you hit or stick?

You stick. In this scenario, you should *always* pass on receiving more cards and hope for the dealer to bust. This holds true even though you may well lose in one of the following ways:

- The dealer could flip over a king and a five, giving her 21.
- You hold and the dealer flips over "your" four. You would have hit 21.
- The dealer could flip over a queen and a three, giving her 19.*

I'll stop here, but plenty of other scenarios would have resulted in your winning, none of which changes the fact that your best bet remains sticking with 17. Conversely, if you are holding a three and a ten (13) and the dealer is showing a queen, you should always hit. Finally, you should always double down on 11.

---

* They call it gambling for a *reason*, right?

 TIP

As even intermediate gamblers know, trust the process, not the outcome.

Prescriptive Analytics

The practice of prescriptive analytics takes its descriptive and predictive counterparts to the next level. Here, numbers go beyond "positive" statements and venture into the world of "normative" ones. Through prescriptive analytics, one can build a model that recommends different courses of action and, critically, shows the likely outcome of each decision. Consider the following example:

- **Descriptive:** As of January 2017, the unemployment rate for blue-collar workers in Texas was currently 11 percent.
- **Predictive:** Based on current macroeconomic trends, there is a 60 percent chance that this number will swell to 13 percent by January 2018.
- **Prescriptive:** By offering a combination of government retraining programs and tax incentives for high-tech organizations, there's a 30 percent chance that the unemployment rate for blue-collar workers in Texas will drop to 8 percent by January 2019.

Note the inherent uncertainty in the last two buckets. There's just no way to know for sure what is going to happen. As the physicist Niels Bohr once opined, "Prediction is very difficult, especially if it's about the future."

STREAMING DATA REVISITED

The previous chapter introduced the related concepts *event-stream processing* (ESP) and *complex event processing* (CEP). (See "Data in Motion" in Chapter 2.) It may seem like semantics or even jargon, but you should never mistake *data at rest* for *data in motion*. This is particularly true with respect to analytics.

As Table 3.3 shows, while similar, the general order of steps required to turn each type of data into meaningful analytics differs.

Table 3.3 Traditional Analytics versus Event-Stream Processing

Traditional Analytics via Data at Rest	Analytics via Event-Stream Processing
1. Receives and stores data, typically from a single source.	1. Stores queries and analysis.
2. Prepares data.	2. Receives data, typically from multiple sources.
3. Processes and analyzes the data.	3. Processes the data.
4. Gets results and *actively* shares as needed.	4. Immediately and *automatically* pushes results.

Source: Adapted from SAS.*

Table 3.3 shows several significant differences between the two processes' respective steps. Traditional analytics could not even begin until the data arrived. The analytics needs to wait on the data. This is not the case with ESP. Here, analytics is queued up, ready to go as soon as the data arrives.

Second, look at the difference regarding step 4. Historically those working with traditional analytics would actively have to communicate their results to others. Because of its speed, ESP often involves triggers and *automatic* notifications not only to people, but also to other systems, data sources, and applications. In other words, ESP may quickly identify threats and opportunities, but that doesn't matter if a person or receiving system doesn't respond to them.

Let's return for a moment to Foursquare, first mentioned in the Preface. Remember that Foursquare's website now describes it as a "location intelligence" company. In and of themselves, those words mean nothing. To be sure, finding real-time and meaningful insights from streaming data requires powerful technology. That's necessary and not sufficient. To finally find profitability under its new model, Foursquare needs third-party developers to build new apps and tap into a range of application program interfaces (APIs) such as Twitter and Google Maps. Fortunately, the company is doing just that via its own API.† As freelance software developer Patrick Klitzke wrote:

> Foursquare API gives us access to a huge database of
> different venues from all around the world. It includes a

---

* See http://bit.ly/2mzVQl9.
† For more on this, see http://bit.ly/1AK3mat.

rich variety of information such as the place's addresses, popularity, tips and photos. The access to the API is available for free and provides an easy setup.[3]

A FINAL WORD ON ANALYTICS

In his book *The Lean Startup*, Eric Ries distinguished between these types of *vanity metrics* versus *actionable* ones.* Unlike the former, the latter offer clear guidance about what to do. An example will illustrate the difference between the two.

Seven years ago, I walked into the offices of a small start-up in New Jersey. I looked at the obligatory whiteboard on the wall and noticed the usual statistics and graphs: number of Twitter followers, Facebook likes, size of the company's mailing list, daily page views, and so on. Sure, these were gradually increasing over time, but what did they really *mean*? Did they help the company acquire customers or understand why this wasn't happening? Remember that not all numbers are useful ones, and these measures did not help the founders make better business decisions.

? TIP

One of the cardinal rules of analytics is that the different types are not all created equal.

CHAPTER REVIEW AND DISCUSSION QUESTIONS

- What are the three main types of analytics?
- Is reporting the same as analytics? What differences exist between the two?
- What does the best analytics do?
- What is data in motion? How does it differ from data at rest?
- What is the point of event-stream processing (ESP)?
- What are different steps involved in deriving traditional and ESP analytics?

---

*I'm not a huge fan of the adjective *actionable*. Many professionals bastardize the term these days, and there's a very specific legal meaning behind it.

NEXT

This chapter concludes Part One. Part Two covers the background and principles of Agile methods, including Scrum. It also provides a general framework for Agile analytics.

NOTES

1. Craig O'Shannessy, "How Hewitt Raised His Level against the Top Players," ATP World Tour, October 26, 2016, http://tinyurl.com/gqktm7n.
2. Jeff Bertolucci, "Big Data Analytics: Descriptive vs. Predictive vs. Prescriptive," *InformationWeek*, December 31, 2013, http://tinyurl.com/ovygdhe.
3. Patrick Klitzke, "Build a Places App with Foursquare and Google Maps Using Onsen UI and AngularJS," Monaca × Onsen Blog, February 4, 2016, http://bit.ly/2mX7JSV.

PART **TWO**

Agile Methods and Analytics

Part One covered the requisite background on data and analytics. Now it's time to introduce Agile methods, and specifically Scrum. In Part Two, you will learn how the Agile world differs markedly from its phase-gate counterpart. To paraphrase Allen Coin, Agile methods are "like finishing a ship while at sea. This way you have to focus on the most important things."*

This part contains the following chapters:

- **Chapter 4:** A Better Way to Work: The Benefits and Core Values of Agile Development
- **Chapter 5:** Introducing Scrum: Looking at One of Today's Most Popular Agile Methods
- **Chapter 6:** A Framework for Agile Analytics: A Simple Model for Gathering Insights

---

* See http://bit.ly/2o52mOD.

A Better Way to Work

The Benefits and Core Values of Agile Development

The secret of getting started is breaking your complex overwhelming tasks into small manageable tasks, and starting on the first one.

—Mark Twain

The dirty little secret in the software industry is that information technology (IT) projects fail more often than not. Sure, not every failure qualifies as a *public spectacle* like the Healthcare.gov debacle, but the track record of Waterfall projects has never been anywhere close to good.

THE CASE AGAINST TRADITIONAL ANALYTICS PROJECTS

In 2014, I spoke at Netflix headquarters about my then-current book, *The Visual Organization*. From the moment I entered the building, I detected a decidedly different vibe compared to that at most organizations on my book tour.

Perhaps it began with the boldly displayed Tech Emmy in the company's lobby.* It continued with the data visualizations on the wall and the employees' profound knowledge of data, analytics, and technology. (I was nowhere near the smartest person in the room.) To be sure, it was an unforgettable experience.

Since that time, I have reflected quite a bit on the two hours I spent at the streaming-video giant. Netflix made quite an impression on me. No wonder that it's one of the most successful companies of the Internet Age. Sure, it built a better mousetrap and benefited from how Blockbuster management grossly misjudged consumer trends. What's more, Netflix has made its fair share of blunders.

REMEMBER QWIKSTER?

In 2011, Netflix announced that it would be effectively splitting its business into two separate services and related websites. Many subscribers would now need to manage two rental queues: one for streaming movies and TV shows, and one for physical DVDs in red envelopes. (For a variety of reasons, don't expect the latter part of Netflix's business to go the way of the dodo anytime soon.) Nearly one million customers promptly canceled their accounts. More took to social media to vent before Reed Hastings abruptly walked back Qwikster.

Ultimately, it was a silly idea. Nonetheless, it proves that Netflix is willing both to take big risks and to listen to data when those risks don't pan out.

---

* For my obligatory selfie, see http://tinyurl.com/zos87j7.

Understandable but Pernicious

The project mentality is prevalent and certainly understandable. It's also pernicious: It encumbers organizations from really embedding analytics into their cultures—something that has never been more essential.

For starters, projects, by definition, need beginning and end dates. Make no mistake: This is a problem in the context of analytics. All too often in my decade working on IT projects, employees would pooh-pooh new responsibilities and ways of working because "things will go back to normal" when the project concludes. This is especially true if the project doesn't go as planned. If you consider that concern trivial, think again. Companies' overall record implementing new technologies is dismal.

Beyond that, a project mind-set contravenes the notion of continuous delivery, something that successful organizations have rightfully adopted for years. Intelligent professionals today recognize that analytics is never "finished." Rather, it needs to be consistently refined, audited, expanded, and even retired when it no longer makes sense.

 TIP

Agile methods are far better suited for analytics precisely because they recognize that the work is never done.

A Different Mind-Set at Netflix

Many organizations continue to approach analytics as a traditional, discrete IT "project" of a finite duration. Netflix, however, certainly does not. My visit to its headquarters in Los Gatos, California, and conversations with its employees corroborated my prior beliefs.

In this regard, among others, Netflix goes against the grain—and it's hard to argue with its results. I'd also put Facebook, Amazon, and Google/Alphabet in the same boat. These companies routinely use analytics to make key business decisions. Put differently, they don't treat analytics as *one-time IT project*. Rather, they consider analytics to be a *business* project that never really ends. They consistently augment their corpuses of knowledge by embracing new data sources. They have built infrastructures that support instant analysis of complex data sources and types, not to mention mind-boggling volumes.

PROVING THE SUPERIORITY OF AGILE METHODS

Over the years, many academics, industry experts, and CIOs have questioned the sanity of blindly continuing to follow failure-laden processes such as the Waterfall method. Expensive consultants armed with proprietary, complex, and fancy-sounding methodologies have often just made things worse. To this end, Agile methods started gaining popularity in the mid-1990s and early 2000s.

Yet, not everyone was on board. Skeptics abounded. Many traditionalists prematurely dismissed Agile methods because they seemed just too, well, weird. Old-school IT folks knew only one way to work. They often had trouble grasping the idea that frequently shipping small batches is even possible, let alone that it almost always beats boiling the ocean. Beyond that, they could think solely in terms of detailed and complicated business requirements, not more pragmatic *user stories*. (We'll cover these in Chapter 5.)

Eager to see how Agile methods compared to their predecessors, Dr. David Rico began studying them in earnest. In 2009, he and his coauthors penned *The Business Value of Agile Software Methods*. The book details the economics of different software-development models. As Dr. Rico et al. described in the text:

> We found 79 studies with quantitative data on the benefits of Agile methods. They cited an average of 26% improvements in cost, 71% improvements in schedule, and 122% improvements in productivity performance. Quality improvements averaged 75% and customer satisfaction improvements averaged 70%. Over 29 of these studies had the data necessary to estimate an average return on investment of 2,633%.

> At least 26 of these studies involving over 726 programmers yielded an average productivity of over 21

lines of code per hour. This is roughly 10 to 20 times the productivity rate associated with traditional methods. At least 21 of these studies involving over 323 programmers yielded an average defect density of about 2 defects per thousand lines of code.

All of these factors combine to make Agile methods more productive to use than traditional methods. Agile methods result in lower maintenance and total life cycle costs due to greater productivity and efficient defect removal. On average, Agile methods are about 25 times more efficient than traditional methods.

Dr. Rico and his colleagues conclusively proved the benefits of Agile methods on software-development projects. He also wondered about teams that formerly worked on phase-gate projects. How did they feel in comparison to their experiences on Agile teams?

Figure 4.1 shows the unequivocal answer to that question through results from internal team surveys. The solid line reflects the scores for Agile teams, while the dashed line reflects teams' scores on Waterfall projects.

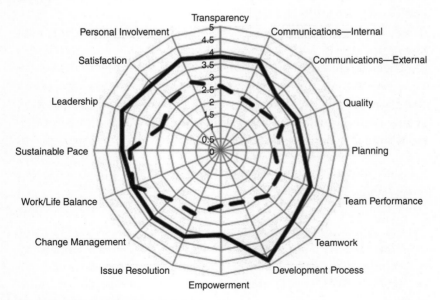

Figure 4.1 Agile Methods: Before and After
Source: The Next Wave of Technologies.

The results could not be clearer. Agile teams report substantial increases along a number of key areas: communications, teamwork, empowerment, team performance, planning, quality, and so on. In fact, Agile methods beat phase-gate methods across the board.

But how exactly does this happen? Is the absence of unrealistic phase-gate deadlines enough? Do Agile teams follow foolproof five-point checklists? Not exactly. The answer lies in *how* Agile teams work.

THE CASE FOR GUIDELINES OVER RULES

Ah, rules. Lovely rules. Where would most companies be without them?

It's a subversive question in many organizations, a sign that you are some type of freethinking anarchist. Still, it's a valid question to ask. After all, rules often don't accomplish what they set out to do. (If you don't believe me, Google *the law of unintended consequences*, a subject that we'll revisit in Chapter 11.) By trying to articulate exactly what is and what is not permitted, organizations allow for massive loopholes, not to mention a general feeling of "management doesn't trust us" by the rank and file.

It's not hard to find instances in which workers may not have violated a specific policy in the employee manual, but their behavior clearly violated its spirit. In a nutshell, this is the problem with rules. So says Dov Seidman in his excellent book *How: Why How We Do Anything Means Everything*. Seidman compellingly argues that conveying general principles governing our behavior is almost always more effective than promulgating myriad rules that forbid specific actions.

That may be fine in theory but a little hokey in practice. Have any organizations made this jump?

As it turns out, yes. A few high-profile companies have realized the inefficiency of trying to manage employee behavior by rules and corporate fiats. For instance, Brazil's Semco S.A. operates in a number of industries, including real estate, banking, and web services. As an organization, its diverse lines of businesses hardly makes it unique. Most of its mainstream press stems from the radical management style that Semco S.A. executives have adopted: The company forgoes traditional management altogether. Instead, employees rely on their own discretion to make almost all decisions.

You may not have heard of Semco S.A., but you probably know of another company that embraces a very different type of management philosophy.

Patty McCord used to serve as chief talent officer at Netflix before hanging out her own shingle. Writing for *Harvard Business Review*, she detailed the ex-employer's über-progressive view on policies (that she helped create):

> We also departed from a formal travel and expense policy and decided to simply require adult-like behavior there, too. The company's expense policy is five words long: "Act in Netflix's best interests." In talking that through with employees, we said we expected them to spend company money frugally, as if it were their own. Eliminating a formal policy and forgoing expense account police shifted responsibility to frontline managers, where it belongs. It also reduced costs.[1]

Scarcity and Trade-Offs on Agile Projects

In his 1932 paper titled "An Essay on the Nature and Significance of Economic Science," Lionel Robbins defined economics as the study of scarcity.[2] It's a remarkably simple definition, yet it makes perfect sense. Governments can't do everything; they have to make choices based on their leaders' priorities. A dollar spent on national defense means one less dollar available for infrastructure improvement or social programs.

The same tenet applies to organizations. Even a colossus such as Amazon cannot pursue each crazy and expensive idea that it considers. It has to make choices about which new products and services to develop. This also applies to divisions, departments, groups, and individuals.

Written in 2001, The Manifesto for Agile Software Development formally codifies the trade-offs inherent in any project. It explicitly states that Agile teams should adhere to the following four principles:

1. **Individuals and interactions** over processes and tools.
2. **Working software** over comprehensive documentation.
3. **Customer collaboration** over contract negotiation.
4. **Responding to change** over following a plan.*

It's easy to read the second of these four tenets and become a little concerned. After all, this is a book on *analytics*, not software development. You need not worry, though. Software development and analytics are more similar than dissimilar. What's more, Agile is, at its core, flexible. As such, we can easily apply the same principles to analytics.

Further, the four tenets do not imply that, for instance, documentation isn't important. It most certainly is, but the Agile Manifesto recognizes that there are only so many hours in a day. As such, *all else being equal*, producing working software—or, in this case, analytics—takes precedence over documenting what you're doing for the future. Ditto for responding to change over following a plan.

The Specific Tenets of Agile Analytics

Making these high-level guidelines and principles explicit increases the chances that Agile methods are ultimately successful. Still, it's not practical to work for months under the vague direction of a four-point doctrine. No, more specific direction is needed in the form of specific precepts. Here, I am borrowing liberally from Ken Collier's excellent book *Agile Analytics*.

- The highest priority is to satisfy the user community through the early and continuous delivery of analytics.
- Agile methods value speed and end-user buy-in over perfection. It's expected and entirely natural for flaws to exist, especially in early stages.
- Agile teams welcome changing requirements, even late in development. This is possible because Agile processes embrace change.

---

* See http://agilemanifesto.org.

- Agile teams deliver analytics frequently. They are often able to integrate new data sources and types every few weeks.

- Everyone on a project must share ownership and work together on a daily basis—not just Scrum teams. This includes stakeholders, end users, developers, analysts, and data scientists.

- Without sufficient trust and resources, Agile teams and projects will fail.

- E-mail generally sucks. It is not a true collaboration tool. Often the best way to brainstorm, convey information, and resolve conflicts is via in-person conversations.

- Agile methods are designed to maximize team productivity, not any one individual's productivity. Local optimization usually causes global degradation.

- Relevant, timely, and *meaningful* analytics is the primary measure of progress.

- The best work often emerges from self-organizing teams.

- There is a fundamental trade-off among a project's scope, schedule, and cost/resources.* For instance, if you reduce the time that a team has to complete a project, then you have to either decrease its scope or provide it with greater resources.

- Agile teams must work at a sustainable pace. Team members need time to think, contemplate, and experiment. When dealing with so much data, the "right" or "best" way may not be readily apparent.

- At regular intervals, Agile teams should reflect on how to become more effective. Single project postmortems offer little value and opportunity to improve.

❷ TIP

If it seems as though keeping a full-time team focused on Agile principles and methods is a full-time job, you're absolutely right. Scrum teams (discussed in the next chapter) hold a specific seat for such a person: the Scrum Master.

---

* A similar maxim is "Fast, cheap, and good: pick any two of the three."

CHAPTER REVIEW AND DISCUSSION QUESTIONS

- Consider Waterfall and Agile methods. When it comes to launching and implementing technology projects, which are generally better and why?
- Are there any circumstances in which the Waterfall method makes sense? If so, what are they? Why do they make sense? If not, why not?
- Why are guidelines generally better than rules?
- What are the four main guidelines from the Agile Manifesto?
- What are some of the specific tenets of Agile methods? How do they differ from older methods?

NEXT

Now that we have established the overarching tenets of Agile projects, it's time to get more specific. The next chapter dives into the ins and outs of one of today's most popular ways of deploying software and analytics: Scrum.

NOTES

1. Patty McCord, "How Netflix Reinvented HR," *Harvard Business Review*, January/February 2014, http://bit.ly/1xrhZjR, retrieved March 11, 2017.
2. Lionel Robbins, "An Essay on the Nature and Significance of Economic Science" (London: Macmillan, 1932).

CHAPTER 5

Introducing Scrum

Looking at One of Today's Most Popular Agile Methods

When you're finished changing, you're finished.

—Benjamin Franklin

A s mentioned in the Introduction, for decades, organizations largely followed Waterfall or phase-gate methods on IT projects. Gantt charts representing one- or two-year timeframes ruled the day. (See Table I.1 in the Introduction.) Failure was common, expensive, and often devastating.

Fortunately, this has started to change. Agile methods are no longer weird. Startups have embraced them for years, but mature organizations are finally starting to see the light. They are opting for smaller batches and Agile methods to further their software-development efforts. In a parallel way, these same organizations' analytics efforts can benefit from adopting a similar mind-set. In a nutshell, this is the premise of this book.

This chapter briefly defines Agile methods, roles, techniques, and terminology with a particular emphasis on Scrum. It is not supposed to be comprehensive. Dozens or even hundreds of books exist on every mainstream Agile method.

❓TIP

Agile analytics is equal parts what you do and how you do it.

A VERY BRIEF HISTORY

The origins of Agile methods date to 1984 when Hirotaka Takeuchi and Ikujiro Nonaka authored a paper in the *Harvard Business Review* entitled "The New New Product Development Game." Takeuchi and Nonaka surveyed several Japanese product-development firms such as Canon, Honda, and NEC Corporation. Their objective: to see why these firms were so successful for so long developing global consumer products.

Whereas U.S. organizations approached projects in very rigid, linear, and phased fashions, their Japanese counterparts did the opposite—that is, they employed cross-functional teams and shorter, more frequent, iterations. The results could not have been more different.

Ken Schwaber and Jeff Sutherland formally codified Scrum in 1995, although the first informal Scrum team was formed in 1993. Today, the Scrum Alliance defines the term as:

> a simple yet incredibly powerful set of principles and practices that help teams deliver products in short cycles, enabling fast feedback, continual improvement, and rapid adaptation to change.*

———————————
* See https://www.scrumalliance.org.

It is "a simple, team-based framework to develop complex systems and products." Note that Scrum is only one type of Agile development method. Other ones include Extreme Programming, Feature-Driven Development, and the Dynamic Systems Development Method. While there are true differences among these approaches, they are more similar than dissimilar.

With the background out of the way, it's now time to introduce the language of Scrum.

SCRUM TEAMS

To paraphrase John Goodman's brilliantly bombastic Walter Sobchak in *The Big Lebowski*, the beauty of a Scrum team lies in its simplicity. Scrum teams consist of only three roles: product owner, Scrum Master, and team member. That's it. Figure 5.1 represents this visually.

Figure 5.1 Simple Visual of Scrum Team Makeup
Source: Phil Simon.

As we'll see in a bit, these roles inhere specific responsibilities; Scrum is not anarchy. Also note that there are no hierarchies—and this is very much by design. Let's say that you are on a Scrum team and your formal job title is *business analyst*. Also on your team is Lydia, your friend's boss and the director of marketing. Lydia may outrank you on the org chart, but for the purposes of the Scrum team, you are equals. Scrum is very egalitarian that way.

Product Owner

The product owner is responsible for maximizing return on investment. She is authorized solely to ask the team to do work and change the priority of product backlog items. She ensures that the team members understand customer needs. She keeps the product vision and prioritizes user stories. Put differently, she is not just another coder.

That's not to say that hers is an easy job. On the contrary, it is often very demanding. She'll often have to deal with issues that run the gamut from legal to compliance to marketing to budgets to management and the like. What's more, the product owner must remain objective while managing any inherent tensions that develop within the team. In the words of Mindi Schnase, project manager for Renown Health and a Certified Scrum Master:

> The product owner should have the type of personality who can "provide the team with high-level requirements and objectives for the product, but will allow the team to determine how to accomplish these goals."*

Finally, the product owner generally writes acceptance criteria. (We'll get to that shortly.)

Scrum Master

The Scrum Master is an expert and advisor, coach, and facilitator. This role is essential for organizations using Scrum for the first time. He may tell the product owner "no." Ideally, he has the maturity, experience, knowledge, and humility to function effectively in this capacity. Put differently, this role might not be a great fit for a 21-year-old recent college graduate who lacks much proper business experience. The Scrum Master occasionally bulldozes impediments. To quote Schnase again:

> If someone can't get into a network folder they need or the testing environment is down, Scrum Masters can help

---

* For more, see http://bit.ly/2mVy5CD.

escalate and resolve these issues. Scrum Masters need to be able to communicate with any stakeholder, in addition to being assertive and enthusiastic.*

If you think that this means being the occasional bad guy, you're right. What's more, Scrum Masters feel a keen sense of ownership over projects. As Mike Cohn, founder of Mountain Goat Software, so eloquently put it:

> An orchestra conductor once explained that he has no real power over how the individual musicians play. Yet he feels a tremendous *responsibility* toward helping them be the best musicians they can be.[1]

Scrum Masters may minimize their involvement as the team coheres, becomes more productive, and increases its understanding of Scrum.

Team Member

On a Scrum team, you'll find far more players than coaches. In other words, team members constitute the majority of Scrum teams. Team members operate with high degrees of authority. They solely determine estimates (i.e., how much time and effort each task takes) and they collaborate freely, and ideally, without regard to title/role.

At bottom, teams and team members face a common objective irrespective of the project: to continue to deliver user stories. That's it. This means maximizing the team's productivity—*not necessarily that of any one individual*. For a team to be effective, a high degree of collaboration needs to exist within a team and among team members. Individuals who are overly possessive about completing "their" user stories often don't want to help others—and the team's productivity suffers for it. This is typically where the Scrum Master steps in.

This brings us to the question of whether teams should be cross-functional. While there's an open debate in the Scrum community about the matter, I'm of the opinion that the answer is yes. In software

---

* Ibid.

development, stacking a team exclusively with programmers often yields disappointing results. It's best to include business analysts and quality-assurance testers as well. Permit me the following analogy: In basketball, 7-foot centers can certainly rebound and block shots, but can they effectively bring the ball up the court? Can they protect the ball from opponents' guards with quick feet and quicker hands?

USER STORIES

For decades, gathering business requirements has been the bane of many IT projects. Fortunately, Scrum explicitly recognizes the futility of this exercise. In its stead, Scrum employs user stories that capture the descriptions of desired features from the point of view of employees, customers, clients, or other end users. In so doing, user stories help create simplified and understandable descriptions of business requirements.

All user stories should contain each of the following three elements:

1. **Role:** Type(s) of users
2. **Goal:** What they want
3. **Benefit:** Why

An example is in order.

On November 30, 2016, Netflix announced that its subscribers could download movies to their devices for future viewing. The next day, I asked two of my students to describe this new feature in the form of a proper user story. Both of them correctly said something along these lines:

> As a Netflix subscriber, I would like the ability to download shows and movies so I can watch them in areas with no or poor network connectivity.

It's important here to describe what proper user stories intentionally omit: *how*. That is, user stories should specify neither the technologies nor the data required to solve the business problem. Scrum team members do this. (Don't worry; we'll return to this subject later in this chapter). Ideally, team members maintain a great deal of autonomy in tackling their user stories.

Clear, concise user stories are essential for all Agile projects—including analytics. Lamentably, many user stories just aren't up to snuff.

❓TIP

Don't confuse user stories with actual tasks. Team members decompose selected user stories into tasks for each sprint. Don't expect to identify all of the tasks ahead of time.

Epics: Too Broad

As evinced by their name, epics are user stories that Scrum teams cannot complete during a single sprint, let alone easily. Epics often combine many smaller user stories into one. You may be wondering why this is a problem. If a user story qualifies as an *epic*, then it falls prey to many of the problems associated with Waterfall projects. Here are two examples of epics:

1. As a supply-chain manager, I need to see all inventory data throughout the company, receive alerts when inventory levels for key products fall below certain thresholds, understand my delivery network via geoanalytics, and view information regarding potential substitutes if weather delays or union issues prevent normal raw-material production.
2. As the head of training and development, I need to view employee survey results in real time to immediately send struggling managers e-mails equipped with links to resources and online training programs. I also need to see which managers have taken which courses and how they performed.

In the first epic, there is no doubt that each of these tasks is important to supply-chain managers. Ditto for the second scenario. However, including each of these tasks in a single user story is a recipe for disaster. It's far better to separate each into several user stories that Scrum teams can complete over the course of one or more sprints.

Too Narrow/Detailed

At the other end of the spectrum are user stories that are far too granular. They include:

1. As the head of sales, I need to view each prospect's name, lead origin, lead date, address, and zip code in an Excel spreadsheet sorted by lead origin so I can run mail merge in Microsoft Word.
2. As the head of analytics, I need the ability to run multivariate regression equations and post the results on my company website, allowing nontechnical users to import the results in Tableau for future visualization and analysis.

Just Right

The following user stories pass the Goldilocks Test—they are neither too broad nor too narrow:

1. As the head of talent management, I need to view attrition rates of high-potential employees to determine whether they are leaving at an accelerated rate.
2. As a bookstore owner, I need to see real-time inventory levels and trends to determine which books to order.

The Spike: A Special User Story

Regardless of their required effort or anticipated complexity, all user stories inhere some degree of risk. Remember that Agile methods explicitly reject the conceit of phase-gate ones: that a project manager or sponsor knows precisely how long each item will take.

But risk is not binary; there are degrees. It's foolish to take core decisions about development frameworks, programming languages, and statistical techniques lightly. Yes, they may not be permanent, but they aren't easily reversed.

In the case of big, risky decisions, *spikes* are very useful. These are specific types of user stories that seek "to gain the knowledge necessary to reduce the risk of a technical approach, better understand a requirement, or increase the reliability of a [user] story estimate."* As Dean Leffingwell wrote in *Agile Software Requirements*:

> Since spikes do not directly deliver user value, they should be used sparingly and with caution.
>
> The output of a spike is demonstrable, both to the team and to any other stakeholders. This brings visibility to research and architectural efforts and also helps build collective ownership and shared responsibility for the key decisions being taken.
>
> And, like any other user story, [the product owner accepts spikes] when the acceptance criteria for the spike have been fulfilled.†

For instance, let's say that your team is trying to decide between competing statistical software packages. On the table are R, SPSS, and SAS Enterprise Miner. This is a big decision and the wrong one will set the firm and the team back months. To avert that very scenario, the product owner invests 40 hours of the team's time in this user story.

BACKLOGS

Product and sprint backlogs underpin Scrum. A *product backlog* lists all desired product features in the form of user stories. (These also go by the names of *backlog items* or just plain *stories*.) The product owner is formally responsible for the product backlog. By definition, it constantly evolves. Items at the top of the backlog tend to be smaller and better defined than those at the bottom. The latter qualify as *nice to have*.

---

* For more on this, see www.scaledagileframework.com/spikes.
† We'll get to acceptance criteria shortly.

The sprint backlog serves as the team's to-do list *for the sprint.* As Figure 5.2 shows, the sprint backlog is a subset of the product backlog.

Figure 5.2 Relationship between Product and Sprint Backlogs
Source: Phil Simon.

Unlike the product backlog, the sprint backlog is finite. The team generates this backlog during sprint planning and it remains the team's focus throughout the duration of the sprint.* Team members may change the tasks required to complete these user stories. However, the user stories themselves should remain constant.

SPRINTS AND MEETINGS

In Scrum, a *sprint* represents the period in which a team completes a predetermined number of user stories. Typically, a sprint lasts one or two weeks. Figure 5.3 displays the general structure of a one-week sprint.

At a high level, Scrum is designed to maximize speed, user acceptance, and, ultimately, the odds of successful outcomes. If this is true, you may be asking, then why do its teams waste so much time in meetings? Nothing could be further from the truth. Each meeting in Figure 5.3 is intended to serve a specific and valuable purpose.

---

*Extreme Programming is another type of Agile development that allows for the sprint backlog to change mid-sprint.

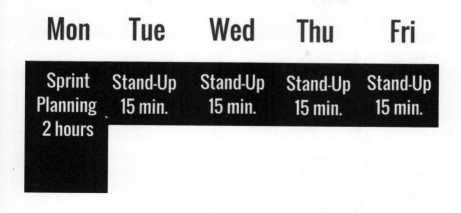

Figure 5.3 Schedule for a One-Week Sprint
Source: Phil Simon.

Sprint Planning

Sprint planning usually takes about two hours. At its core, the meeting seeks to achieve two things: a sprint goal and a sprint backlog. That's it.

The product owner and team members shouldn't develop and agree on verbose and complicated goals. Rather, goals are ideally short, one- or two-sentence descriptions of what the team plans to achieve during the sprint.

The sprint backlog reflects the specific user stories that the team commits to completing during the sprint. Team members should begin thinking about the specific tasks they need to complete to deliver the agreed-on user stories. Note that the product owner doesn't assign tasks akin to what a traditional project manager would. Scrum is supposed to be collaborative. Think conversations, not fiats.

Daily Stand-Up

Also known as *daily scrums*, teams hold these mandatory 15-minute daily meetings in the morning. These meetings should be brief and focused. If you wonder why it's called a *stand-up*, remember that meetings tend to outlive their utility when people are comfortable (read: sitting down).

Each team member should quickly answer the following three questions:

1. What did you do yesterday?
2. What will you do today?
3. Are there any impediments in your way?*

Goals here include transparency and problem identification; the stand-up is neither a traditional status meeting nor a technical discussion. Should team members start pontificating or losing focus, the Scrum Master should intervene.

Story Time

Also known as *backlog grooming*, this optional meeting typically takes place when the sprint is a little more than halfway complete. The goal is also straightforward: to maintain small and well-understood user stories at the top of the backlog at all times. Without such user stories, the team will likely lose momentum when the next sprint begins. Note that the focus of this meeting should be *upcoming* user stories, not the ones in the current sprint.

Demo

For Scrum team members, this is usually the most enjoyable part of the sprint. Here the team shows off its work to stakeholders—that is,

---

*For a more detailed description, see http://bit.ly/2nkjNvm.

people who do *not* work on the Scrum team. Goals include maximizing transparency and gaining stakeholder trust. By showing each iteration of the product development, stakeholders are less likely to be surprised at the final release compared to phase-gate projects.

Sprint Retrospective

Scrum beats phase-gate methods across the board, but it certainly isn't perfect—no method, project, or team is. Scrum is designed to practice what it preaches: to not only launch the "product" more efficiently, but also to improve the process and efficiency of the team.

In the second vein, the sprint retrospective is crucial. It attempts to answer the following three high-level questions:

1. What did we learn during the sprint?
2. What went wrong during the sprint?
3. How can we improve next time?

Note that this meeting is not supposed to serve as a gripe session. Scrum Masters should ensure that team members express all issues in a professional way.

RELEASES

Typically, each product or model release consists of several sprints. That is, after two or three weeks of completing user stories, the team has developed sufficient features to justify a new version. It's time to release the new iteration into the wild so others can enjoy the fruits of the team's labor.

Aside from regular or scheduled releases, other factors may come into play when determining releases:

- **Date:** E-commerce sites and apps pay particular attention to Cyber Monday, Mother's Day, and Valentine's Day.
- **Functionality:** If a competitor launches a killer feature, a product owner may prioritize new user stories to staunch the bleeding.

■ **Exigent circumstances:** Users discover a key problem or bug that warrants immediate attention. This often pushes back previously scheduled user stories.

Each of these departures is acceptable. Unlike the Waterfall method, Scrum is designed to handle unforeseen changes and crises.

ESTIMATION TECHNIQUES

Generally speaking, Waterfall projects suffer from the difficulty of estimating how long individual tasks—let alone entire phases—will take. This dooms many projects from the start. For instance, will it take three or four months to *collect, clean, deduplicate,* and *load* enterprise data into a new business-intelligence tool or data warehouse? Even a modest 20 percent delay in one step of a phase-gate project affects all other phases, immediately rendering the project significantly behind schedule.

Agile methods such as Scrum avoid this all-too-real scenario in several ways. First, through sprints, Scrum teams work to complete tasks in small batches, not large ones. In this case, the team first completes user stories around *collecting* data—and only a certain type of data at that. Perhaps it first tackles customer data and then proceeds to product or employee data. By breaking work into more manageable parts, Scrum teams tend to be far more successful than their Waterfall counterparts.

But Scrum teams excel for another reason: the superior nature of their estimates. More specifically, Scrum teams rely on *relative* estimates—not *absolute* ones. A simple, nontechnical example illustrates the point.

On Lawns and Relative Estimates

I recently moved into a new home in Arizona not too far from Arizona State University's Tempe campus. I had lived outside of Las Vegas, Nevada, for the prior five years. My new backyard is about half as large as my old one, and with real grass on half of it. (I prefer it to its artificial equivalent.) Figure 5.4 shows a simple diagram.

Nevada   **Arizona**

Figure 5.4 Simple Representation of Grass at Author's Former and Current Home
Source: Phil Simon.

As I prepared to mow my new lawn in March for the first time, I didn't know how exactly long it would take. I did know, however, that it would take less time than it took for me to mow the lawn at my Nevada home. In other words, I used a relative estimate and I was right.

This doesn't make me exceptional; it makes me a human being. We are generally terrible at making absolute estimates, but adept at making relative ones. We can effectively differentiate between and among items with one caveat: the items need to be sufficiently disparate. If I were standing on the ground and looking up at two buildings, I wouldn't necessarily be able to tell which one was taller; it all depends on the height of the buildings and my proximity to them. In Figure 5.5, the two buildings are dissimilar enough that, even in an era of alternative facts, any sober adult can tell that the one on the left is much larger.

Figure 5.5 Two Very Different Buildings
Source: Phil Simon.

But what about the buildings shown in Figure 5.6? Would you be able to tell which one is taller if you were standing near the entrance of one of them?

Figure 5.6 Two Very Similar Buildings
Source: Phil Simon.

No, you would be guessing. The buildings aren't sufficiently different.

Fibonacci Numbers

It turns out that this concept dates all the way back to an Italian mathematician named Leonardo of Pisa (aka Fibonacci). In his 1202 text *Liber Abaci*, he introduced the eponymous Fibonacci sequence:

$$0 + 1 = 1$$
$$1 + 1 = 2$$
$$1 + 2 = 3$$
$$2 + 3 = 5$$
$$3 + 5 = 8$$
$$5 + 8 = 13$$
$$8 + 13 = 21$$

As you can see, Fibonacci numbers get big quickly; the numbers in the sequence are meant to denote differences in a way that humans can easily discern. For instance, 3 is 50 percent greater than 2. The number 13 is 62.5 percent greater than 8. Figure 5.7 shows the first few numbers of the sequence in a graphical form.

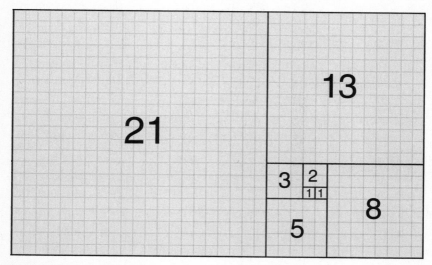

Figure 5.7 Fibonacci Sequence
Source: By 克勞棟—Own work, CC BY-SA 4.0.*

Note that in Scrum, Fibonacci numbers also go by the moniker *story points*.

T-Shirt Sizes

Some Scrum teams prefer to use T-shirt sizes in lieu of Fibonacci numbers for relative estimates. In this case, small, medium, large, and extra large replace 8, 13, 21, and so on. As we'll see in Chapter 7, some of my students did this very thing when working with the University Tutoring Center on their semester-long capstone project.

---

* https://commons.wikimedia.org/w/index.php?curid=38708516.

When Teams Disagree

For several reasons, Scrum teams tend to be inherently more collaborative than their counterparts on Waterfall projects. For one, the former are more egalitarian. With only three roles, formal job titles don't matter—*or at least they shouldn't*. As a result, there's less chance for politics, especially as teams congeal. Second, Scrum teams generally consist of five to nine members. Finally, team members are supposed to work with a great deal of autonomy. User stories describe what employees want; they do not mandate *how* to deliver specific features.

That's not to say, though, that team members don't disagree from time to time. This is fairly common with newer teams. When this happens, the teams typically play either Planning Poker or the Team Estimation Game. Both are simple yet effective ways to resolve conflicts.

Planning Poker

Let's say that Dinesh, Gilfoyle, and Nelson disagree on the number of points to assign to a user story.* Table 5.1 represents their honest estimates.

Table 5.1 Estimates for User Story Points

Team Member	Estimate
Dinesh	8
Gilfoyle	5
Nelson	21

Source: Phil Simon.

Other team members include Erlich (product owner), Jared (Scrum Master), and Richard, Russ, and Monica (all team members).

To start, each estimator receives separate cards with the estimates of Dinesh, Gilfoyle, and Nelson. For the user story, Erlich reads the description of the user story. He also moderates a discussion and answers questions.

After discussion, Richard, Russ, and Monica each select cards representing their guesses. The three then concurrently flip them over.

---

* This is a not-so-subtle nod to the hysterical HBO series *Silicon Valley*.

Now all participants can see each other's estimates. Table 5.2 shows their selections.

Table 5.2 Planning Poker, Round 1

Team Member	Estimate
Richard	5
Monica	8
Russ	21

Source: Phil Simon.

Because their estimates are the highest and lowest, respectively, Richard and Russ explain their points of view. Erlich takes notes. After discussion, the team repeats the process. As is often the case, the team quickly reaches consensus, shown in Table 5.3.

Table 5.3 Planning Poker, Round 2

Team Member	Estimate
Richard	5
Monica	5
Russ	21

Source: Phil Simon.

Team Estimation Game

Another way to quickly reach agreement involves placing user stories in order of perceived difficulty or amount of work. This jibes nicely with our innate ability to accurately make *relative* estimates, if not absolute ones.

Erlich selects 20 stories from the product backlog. He writes them down on index cards or Post-it notes. Finally, he distributes them equally to the team members.

Dinesh begins the game by picking out a user story and placing it on the whiteboard, arranged by perceived story size. Russ goes next with his first user story. He thinks that his requires more points than Dinesh's, but Gilfoyle disagrees. A skilled coder, he can complete it much quicker than Russ can. Russ moves his user story closer to the left.

This process repeats until something similar to Figure 5.8 eventually begins to take shape.

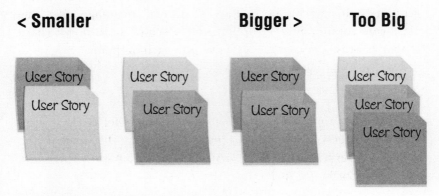

Figure 5.8 Team Estimation Game, Round 1
Source: Figure from Phil Simon.

When everyone agrees with how the user stories rank, it's time to tidy up. The team completes the game by assigning Fibonacci numbers to each column. In the end, the whiteboard looks something like Figure 5.9.

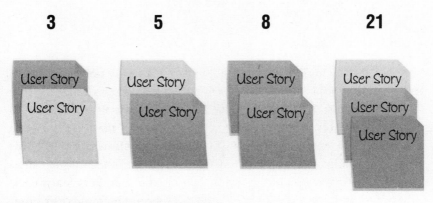

Figure 5.9 Team Estimation Game, Round 2
Source: Figure from Phil Simon.

It's not uncommon for a Scrum team to breeze through 20 or more user stories in an hour. As an added benefit, the game often creates a positive dynamic among group members.

OTHER SCRUM ARTIFACTS, TOOLS, AND CONCEPTS

Scrum teams not only benefit from employing superior estimation techniques. Its practitioners enjoy a distinct advantage over their phase-gate counterparts in the form of velocities, burn-down charts, Kanban boards, and more. Let's delve into each of them.

Velocities

A sprint's velocity simply represents the total number of story points from completed user stories. For instance, let's say that a team completes four user stories during its first sprint. Table 5.4 shows the team's velocity for sprint number 1.

Table 5.4 Sample Points for User Story and Sprint Velocity

User Story	Points
1	5
2	8
3	5
4	3
Sprint Velocity	**23**

Source: Phil Simon.

This begs a chicken-and-egg question: How many points' worth of user stories should a team attempt to complete during a sprint?

It's wise to start conservatively. There's no sense in committing to obscene estimates. After completing the first sprint, the team may still not know how much it can realistically accomplish next time. If this happens, it helps to use prior velocities as a guide, a technique called *yesterday's weather*. Finally, as teams cohere and members learn each others' strengths and weaknesses, velocities should increase over time.

Burn-Down Charts

A burn-down chart graphically reflects each sprint's velocities. Figure 5.10 shows a sample burn-down chart.

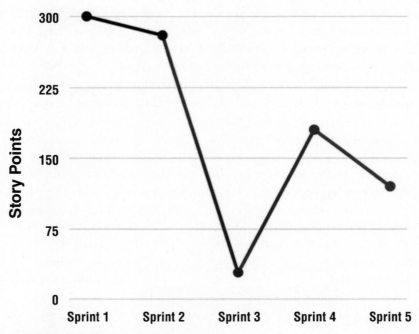

Figure 5.10 Generic Burn-Down Chart
Source: Figure from Phil Simon.

Figure 5.10 is simple by design. It does not show any increases in total story points associated with the project or launch. In reality, though, this happens frequently as a product owner adds more user stories to the product backlog. Remember that Scrum does not require teams to gather all user stories prior to commencing.

Also note in Figure 5.10 that the slope of the line increases over time—technically, the slope becomes more negative. This happens because, as mentioned earlier, team velocities tend to increase over time.

Definition of Done and Acceptance Criteria

Your team has completed a task, but how do you really know that it's really done? More important, does everyone agree that that task is, in fact, finished?

For this very reason, a shared definition of *done* is essential. In the software-development world, it usually means that something is ready to ship. This is an end, and *done* probably includes both code and design reviews as well as different types of testing. Let's say that a team member completes a user story by adding some new code. That addition, however, breaks other key features of a product. Is that new user story really done after all?

Think of acceptance criteria as cousins of *done*. Moreover, they are the conditions that a software product must satisfy to be accepted by a user, customer, or a receiving system. Note that you can't get a little bit pregnant. There is no such thing as *partial acceptance*: a criterion is either met or it is not.

Kanban Boards

On long Waterfall projects, project managers typically relied on Microsoft Project and very involved Gantt charts. Together, they offered the illusion of predictability and control. I can't say that either tool is inherently unhelpful or confusing, but neither allows team members to easily understand what's going on.

By way of contrast, a simple Kanban board can effectively convey the status of user stories and tasks on a sprint.* Figure 5.11 shows a sample.

To Do	In Progress	Done	Tested
Build first iteration of model	Clean customer data	Test connection to Twitter API	Test connection to Oracle dB

Figure 5.11 Sample Kanban Board for Analytics Project
Source: Phil Simon.

---

* For more on Kanban boards' many benefits and the rationale behind using them, see http://bit.ly/2mNVCn6.

Many Scrum teams use physical Kanban boards made up of different colors of index cards. This type of decidedly low-tech method is especially common when team members are colocated. It may seem odd, but individuals often enjoy the process of physically moving a task or user story from the "in process" column to the "done" column. For distributed or virtual teams, many project-management applications such as Trello* allow the same movement among columns.

CHAPTER REVIEW AND DISCUSSION QUESTIONS

- What are the three roles on Scrum teams? What does each do?
- What are user stories? Why are they important? What are their three parts?
- Which is more accurate: relative or absolute estimates? Why?
- What is a burn-down chart? What should its general direction be?
- Should sprint velocities increase or decrease over time? Why?
- Why are Kanban boards helpful?

NEXT

Chapters 4 and 5 introduced Agile methods and Scrum. Before concluding Part Two, it's time to broach one last important concept: a framework for tying this all together.

---

* See http://bit.ly/2nbAN8Q.

A Framework for Agile Analytics

A Simple Model for Gathering Insights

If I can't picture it, I can't understand it.

—Albert Einstein

A t least in the software-development world, Agile methods are old hat today. Companies such as Amazon, Google, Facebook, Apple, Twitter, Microsoft, and countless others in the technology sector have long recognized the superiority of Scrum compared to the Waterfall method. Based on the success of these companies and the need to adapt quickly to a remarkably dynamic business environment, Agile methods have penetrated other industries.

Founded in 1892 in Schenectady, New York, General Electric (GE) is one of the oldest and most storied enterprises in the world. In a way, though, that doesn't matter. As former executives at Black-Berry, Kodak, and Blockbuster can attest, previous success does not guarantee future success. To adapt to the realities of the twenty-first century, GE's management recognized the need to get with the times—and, increasingly, this means adopting Agile practices, such as Scrum.

Consider Brad Surak, now GE Digital's Chief Operating Officer (COO). Surak began his career as a software engineer. As such, he

> was intimately familiar with Agile. He piloted Scrum with the leadership team responsible for developing industrial Internet applications and then, more recently, began applying it to the new unit's management processes, such as operating reviews.[1]

Although the notion of Agile analytics is relatively new, it is quickly gaining steam. As Part Three shows, organizations are using data and analytics to solve a wide variety of business problems. Before we arrive at proper case studies, we've got some work to do.

This brief chapter provides a *simple* and *general* framework for gleaning insights in an iterative or Agile fashion. The framework displayed in Figure 6.1 seeks to avoid the costly mistakes of Waterfall analytics projects.

Even at a high level, the intent here should be obvious: You should not attempt to analyze every conceivable data source in one large batch. You'll be much better served by completing a series of smaller batches. Ditto for spending months attempting to build the perfect model.

 TIP

Don't try to boil the ocean.

Let's cover each of these steps in a fair amount of detail.

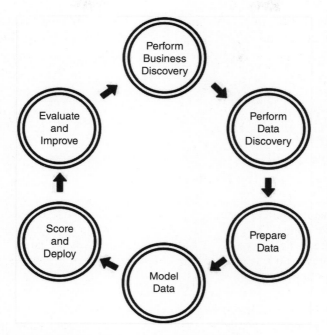

Figure 6.1 A Simple Six-Step Framework for Agile Analytics
Source: Model adapted from Alt-Simmons' book Agile by Design. *Figure created by Phil Simon.*

PERFORM BUSINESS DISCOVERY

Analytics doesn't exist in a vacuum. Sure, at some intellectual level you may wonder why your customers are churning or you can't accurately predict inventory levels at your company. Still, at this point, hopefully you are attempting to solve a real business problem, not conduct an interesting but largely academic exercise.

To that end, you should start with key questions such as the following:

- What are we trying to achieve?
- What behavior(s) are we trying to understand, influence, and/ or predict?

- What type of data would we need to address these issues?*
- Is the project even viable?
- Does our organization possess the time, budget, and resources to undertake the project?
- Is our organization committed to the project? Or will the project fade into the background as more important priorities crop up?
- What happens if we don't answer these questions? What if the project takes longer than expected?

At this point, members of your team may very well disagree about the answers to some of these questions. For instance, not everyone may concur about whether the project is even viable. Disagreement is healthy as long as it is respectful.

To assess the viability of any analytics endeavor, it's wise to hold discovery workshops. These brainstorming sessions can flush out ideas. Perhaps Saul is a skeptic because he saw a similar organizational project fail five years ago. He doesn't realize that new leadership, technologies, data sources, and business realities have changed the game. Maybe Penny is a Pollyanna because this is her first project and she just assumes that everyone will follow her lead.

Resist the urge to skip this step. Next, try to start with a testable hypothesis or working theory of why a problem is occurring. For instance:

- **Initial hypothesis:** Customers are leaving because our products are too expensive.
- **Null hypothesis:** Customers are not leaving because our products are too expensive.

Don't worry about completely answering this question from the get-go. Remember that this is a cycle. You'll have plenty of time to introduce additional hypotheses, variables, and data sources. Odds are that a single simple hypothesis won't explain the entirety of the business problem that you're addressing in this stage anyway.

---

* We'll get to whether that data exists in the next phase.

PERFORM DATA DISCOVERY

If you're of a certain age, as I am, you remember a much different data landscape 20 years ago. Across the board, individuals and companies accessed far less data when making decisions. In a way, this made decision making easier. For instance, employees didn't have to worry about collecting and analyzing data from social networks because they didn't exist. The World Wide Web was just getting started. You couldn't answer as many questions as comprehensively as you can today—at least in theory.

Today, we have the opposite problem. The arrival of Big Data means that discovery has never been more important. Critical data-related questions include:

- Where does the desired data "live"?
- Is it even available?
- Is it legal to use? Is it free to use?
- Are we able to retrieve the data in a clean and usable format? Or do we need to scrape it using one of the tools mentioned earlier? (See "Getting the Data" in Chapter 2.)
- Is use of the data restricted? (For instance, Twitter limits access to its firehouse. The company intentionally throttles users who attempt to access too much data, especially first-time users.)
- Can you pay to circumvent those restrictions? How much?
- How long will it take to access/acquire the data?
- How old is our data? Has it aged well?
- If the data exists inside of the enterprise, which organizations and departments own the data? Are they willing to share it with you? (Don't assume that the answer is yes.)
- Is the data complete, accurate, and deduplicated?

At this point, it's wise to remember Douglas Hofstadter's wonderfully recursive law: "It always takes longer than you expect, even when you take into account Hofstadter's Law."* Avoid committing to overly aggressive timelines for analytics. Remember that perfect is the enemy of good.

---

*For more, see http://bit.ly/2m2p7pF.

Also, know going in that it's unlikely that you'll solve your problem via a single data source, no matter how robust or promising it is. Start with what you know, but expect surprises. If a finding doesn't surprise you at some point, then you're probably not looking hard enough. Recognize that you're never going to get all the desired data.

Finally, it's wise at this point to digest the data that you have unearthed for a little while. Remember spikes (which are discussed in Chapter 5). Yes, you can always restart your efforts, but you won't recoup the time. Agile methods such as Scrum don't include time machines.

PREPARE THE DATA

Odds are that your data will contain at least a few errors, inconsistencies, and omissions, especially at first. Data quality isn't sexy, but it's a really big deal. In fact, data preparation may take a great deal of time and prevent you from getting started in earnest. You'll probably need to parse, scrub, collect, and manipulate some data. Consider the following example.

In one of my Enterprise Analytics classes, a group of my students agreed to help a local retail business analyze its data against industry benchmarks. (I call the small business *A1A* here.) My students thought that they would be receiving pristine data in a format to which they had become accustomed. In other words, they thought that A1A's data would be transactional (i.e., long, not wide). Table 6.1 shows the expected format.

As Table 6.1 shows, each transaction exists as a proper record in a sales table. (This is the way that contemporary systems store transactional data.) Lamentably, my students learned that A1A kept its data in the antiquated format demonstrated in Figure 6.2.

Table 6.1 Expected Client Data

Customer_ID	PurchDate	PurchAmt	ProductCode
1234	1/1/08	12.99	ABC
1234	1/19/08	14.99	DEF
1234	1/21/08	72.99	XYZ

Source: Phil Simon.

Table 6.2 contains the same data as Table 6.1, but this isn't a potato-po-tah-toe situation. Each table represents the data in a very different way. Note that storing data in this manner was much more common in the 1980s. (For more on this, see "How Much? Kryder's Law" in Chapter 1.)

Table 6.2 Actual Client Data

Customer_ID	Purch Date1	Purch Amt1	Product Code1	Purch Date2	Purch Amt2	Product Code2
1234	1/1/08	12.99	ABC	1/19/08	14.99	DEF
1235	1/1/12	72.99	XYZ	1/19/08	14.99	DEF
1236	1/1/08	12.99	ABC	1/19/08	72.99	XYZ

Source: Phil Simon.

By way of background, A1A hired temps to manually enter its sales data in Microsoft Excel. Not unexpectedly, the temps lacked a background in system design and data management. As such, they kept adding new columns (technically, *fields*) to the spreadsheet. This may seem like an inconsequential difference, but from a data perspective, it most certainly was not. If a customer booked 200 sales over the years with A1A, then the spreadsheet would contain more than 600 different fields with no end in sight. While the current version of Excel supports more than 16,000 different fields,* A1A's data was, quite frankly, unwieldy.

My students had to wade through hundreds of columns to transform the data into a far more usable and current format. Transposing data is time consuming. What's more, this was not the only issue related to the data's structure. As a result of their discoveries, the students spent the majority of the semester rebuilding A1A's database from scratch. They couldn't get to what they considered the good stuff (read: the analytics) until the very end of the project.

When preparing data for analytics, ask yourself the following key questions:

- Who or what generates the data? (Remember from Chapter 1 the burgeoning Internet of Things. A machine may generate the data, but that doesn't mean that the data is completely accurate.)

---

* See http://bit.ly/2nu46RU.

- If people are responsible for generating the data, are they trained in how to enter it properly? Was there turnover in the organization that could introduce inconsistencies and errors?
- Is the data coming directly from the system of record or from another source, such as a data mart or data warehouse?
- How is the data currently generated and has that ever changed?
- How much data is generated?
- What if the data is flawed or incomplete? What are the downsides?
- Is certain data absolutely required to proceed? What types of proxies can we use if we are left with no choice?
- How complex is the data?
- How frequently is the data updated?

❷ TIP

Often, heat maps, simple SQL statements, pivot tables, histograms, and basic descriptive statistics can provide valuable insights into the state of your data. A day of data preparation may save you six weeks' time down the road.

MODEL THE DATA*

Many professionals are afraid of building models, and some of my students are a little apprehensive as well. I understand the hesitation. After all, it sounds a little daunting. What happens if you get it wrong?

Here's the rub: As George E. P. Box once said, "Essentially, all models are wrong, but some are useful."

❷ TIP

The question isn't whether a model is completely accurate; no model is. The real question hinges on whether a model is *useful*.

---

* Note that I use the terms *forecasting, modeling,* and *predictive analytics* interchangeably.

At a high level, the goal of any model is to understand, describe, and/or predict an event. (See "Types of Analytics" in Chapter 3.) This holds true whether you are trying to predict customer churn, the most relevant search results, or, as we'll see shortly, basketball outcomes.

Taking a step back, you want to know the following:

- Which variables are important
- The absolute and relative importance of these variables
- Which variables ultimately don't matter

In a business context, most models lead—or at least *should* lead—to specific actions designed to improve business outcomes. To this end, the model may focus on customers, prospects, employees, users, or partners.

ADVICE ON BUILDING MODELS

I'm fond of metaphors. For instance, IT projects are like landing planes. It's best to slowly ease into a landing, not try to stop on a dime.

Along the same lines, I often analogize data and analytics endeavors to building houses. Let's say that you hire an architect to build a duplex. As your house starts to become a reality, you decide that you don't need a fourth bedroom after all. Remove the closet and voilà! It's an office.

Most structural changes, however, aren't feasible past a certain point. There's no way to inexpensively turn that duplex into a ranch without starting from scratch. Keep the house analogy in mind when creating models.

Beyond that, ensure that your modeling software handles additional volumes and types of data. What's more, your program of choice should accommodate additional complexity should you choose to add it. Different tools and programming languages are better suited for different data types and sizes than others.

The Power of a Simple Model

Many books tackle building models, and I won't attempt to summarize them here. (Remember, this book emphasizes breadth over depth.) For now, heed the following advice: It's best to start simply, especially at first. Fight the urge to overcomplicate initial models. As the following anecdote illustrates, models need not be terribly sophisticated to bear fruit.

 # RELIVING THE 1997 NCAA TOURNAMENT

For decades, millions of Americans have filled out brackets for the National Collegiate Athletic Association (NCAA) Men's College Basketball Tournament. In 1997, the World Wide Web was exploding and ESPN.com made "bracketology" easier than ever. For the first time, you could submit your brackets online and see how your picks compared against those of everyone else in the world. Oh, the technology!

At the time, I was finishing up my graduate degree at Cornell University. I didn't know much about college basketball, but I knew a few things about data and building models. With graduation looming and my future full-time job secured, I wasn't lacking for free time. (Ithaca, New York, is chilly in March, and I don't ski.) I asked a bunch of my friends if they were interested in participating in a different type of NCAA pool.

Ten of them agreed, and on Wednesday, March 12, 1997, we drafted players in a serpentine order. (The 64-team tournament started on Thursday.) Under snake drafts, the person with the first pick selects and then waits until the end of the second round for his next slot—the 20th overall. He would then pick the 21st player and then not again until the 40th selection. The person with the second pick would have to wait until the 19th to go again and so forth.

Tournament Rules

Rather than attempt to predict which *teams* advanced in each round, I asked my friends if they wanted to kick in $15 each in a *player*-based tournament.

Players' scores would represent the total of their points, rebounds, and assists. Players would accumulate points as long as their teams remained alive. If their teams lost, then they could no longer add to their teams' totals because they no longer suited up. Whichever team had the highest combination of points at the end of the tournament would win the $150 prize. All points, rebounds, and assists counted as one point each. A 20-point scorer would count for as many points as a 10-point scorer who grabbed 10 rebounds per game.

Draft Strategy

In their quests to win the prize, my friends employed very qualitative approaches. That is, they picked the players whom they recognized, even if they played for teams expected to lose in the first round.

I did not.

I didn't care if a player was fundamentally better than any other. I only cared about expected values. For instance, a star like Tim Duncan of Wake Forest (a number-three seed) was certainly valuable, but I only expected him to play three games. In the third round, Wake Forest would most likely play a number-two seed. (Although exceptions abound, higher-seeded teams have tended to beat lower-seeded ones throughout the tournament's history.)

Getting the Data

I downloaded each player's season statistics from ESPN.com and built a simple model in Microsoft Excel. I then started ranking players. For instance, let's say that Duncan averaged 20 points, eight rebounds, and five assists per game over three tournament games. His expected value would be 99: $[(20 + 8 + 5) \times 3]$. Duncan ultimately played only two tournament games that year as Stanford (a number-six seed) knocked off Wake Forest 72–66. Duncan only accounted for 92 points.* Bawdy numbers, but hardly worthy of a top-three pick. (My model projected that he would account for 116.1 total points over three games, 26.1 percent *lower* than his final score.)

If this sounds complicated, I assure you that it wasn't. It took me a little more than an hour to download the data, build my model, and project player expected values.

The Draft: My Model in Action

With my first-round pick I grabbed Bobby Jackson, a guard from the University of Minnesota. No surprise there. Jackson averaged 19.4 points, 7.4 rebounds, and three assists that year. Most important, the Golden Gophers earned a number-one seed in the Midwest Regional. I

---

* In two games, Duncan actually averaged 22 points, 22 rebounds, and two assists.

(*Continued*)

expected Jackson to play at least five games for me, and in the process, accrue a boatload of points.

In the fifth round, I selected Scott Padgett of Kentucky. Padgett was nowhere near as skilled as Jackson, never mind Duncan, a college stud and future NBA immortal. Still, Padgett's stats were, put kindly, understated. In the 1996–1997 season, over 32 games, he averaged 9.6 points, 5.1 rebounds, and 1.8 assists (16.5 total). This was respectable, but hardly worthy of a first- or even third-round pick. Best of all, Padgett flew well under my friends' radar.* He should not have even been available when I snagged him in the fifth round.

I had my eye on Padgett, though, because that year Kentucky was ranked first in the West Regional. Number-one seeds are the most likely to advance to the Final Four. In so doing, they play five games minimum and more if they advance to the championship game. If Padgett only suited up for five games, my model predicted that he would net me 82.5 total points. (Remember that, all else being equal, more games equal more points.)

When I grabbed Padgett with my fifth-round pick, my friends chuckled. After all, Padgett was decent but hardly an elite player. No bother. I didn't care about his objective basketball skills; I only cared about his projected points under my model. (For my part, I was silently laughing at their silly picks; they grabbed players with high name recognition but low expected values.)

Why I Will Buy Scott Padgett Dinner if I Ever Meet Him

It turns out that I had the last laugh with my friends. My remarkably simple model netted me the $150 prize.

In 1997, Kentucky lost to Arizona in the NCAA Championship. Padgett played in seven total games. In the process, he netted me 129 points, nearly 56 percent more than what my model had predicted. (I didn't even need his final-game contribution in the Arizona game; I had cinched my victory and all the other players on my friends' teams had been eliminated.)

---

* Not that I know nearly as much as he does about analytics, but it turns out that Billy Beane was employing a similar philosophy at the same time as general manager of the Oakland A's.

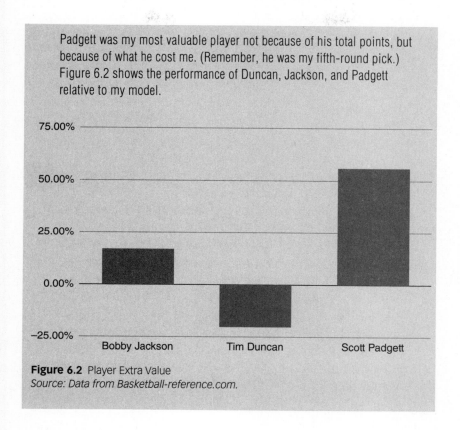

Padgett was my most valuable player not because of his total points, but because of what he cost me. (Remember, he was my fifth-round pick.) Figure 6.2 shows the performance of Duncan, Jackson, and Padgett relative to my model.

Figure 6.2 Player Extra Value
Source: Data from Basketball-reference.com.

There are two morals of my little yarn. First, models need not be complicated to be effective. Why not start with Occam's razor? Second, to succeed you still need to get a little lucky. As Branch Rickey once wrote, "Luck is the residue of hard work and design."

Forecasting and the Human Factor

Up until now, this book has emphasized the decidedly nonhuman components of data and analytics. To be sure, awareness of data types and structures, the different types of analytics, and the framework discussed in this chapter are critical. Put differently, absent this knowledge it's nearly impossible to attain any *sustainable* level of success with analytics. (Of course, there's always dumb luck.)

Before proceeding, it's critical to accentuate a decidedly human point. A note from the Introduction bears repeating: Data and analytics generally do not make decisions by themselves. We human beings do, and we *can* act in a deliberate way that will maximize our odds of success. (Part Three shows how much leadership and openness to analytics drive successful outcomes.)

Philip Tetlock is an Annenberg University Professor at the University of Pennsylvania. For 20 years, he studied the accuracy of thousands of forecasts from hundreds of experts in dozens of fields. His 2005 book *Expert Political Judgment* examined why these alleged "experts" so frequently made wildly inaccurate predictions in just about every field.*

In 2011, Tetlock began The Good Judgment Project along with Barbara Mellers and Don Moore. The multiyear endeavor aimed to forecast world events via the wisdom of the crowd. Think of them as *forecasting tournaments* with mystifying results: Predictions from nonexperts were "reportedly 30 percent better than intelligence officers with access to actual classified information."[2]

Understanding Superforecasters

Intrigued by this discovery, Tetlock and Dan Gardner wrote a 2015 follow-up book, *Superforecasting: The Art and Science of Prediction*. Tetlock wanted to know why a very small percentage of people routinely performed exceptionally well, even in areas in which they lacked any previous knowledge. He called this group of people *superforecasters*.

Table 6.3 shows some of the differences between superforecasters and their regular brethren.

Brass tacks: Let's say that you need to solve a problem of relative sophistication. You give the same data to groups of superforecasters and vanilla experts. As a result of their mind-sets, the former is far more likely to produce a superior solution than the latter. To paraphrase Isaiah Berlin's essay, foxes are better than hedgehogs.

---

*This was the basis for one of my favorite talks in my public-speaking days, "I'm an Expert. Don't Trust Me." Watch it at http://bit.ly/2nywOV6.

Table 6.3 Regular Forecasters versus Superforecasters

Regular Forecasters	Superforecasters
Myopic and provincial. They tend to start with an inside view and rarely look outside. These folks generally can't get away from their own predispositions and attachments.	Ignorant in a good way. They tend to start with an outside view and slowly adopt an inside view. That is, they look heavily at external data sources, news articles, and crowd indicators, especially as starting points.
Lazy. They doubt that there is interesting data lying around.	Stubborn. They believe strongly that there is interesting data lying around, even if they can't quickly find it.
Tend to rely on informed hunches and make the data conform to those hunches.	Engage in active, open-minded thinking. They go wherever the data takes them, even if it contradicts their preexisting beliefs.
Tend to believe in fate.	Tend to reject fate and understand that someone has to win. Examples here include lotteries, markets, poker tournaments, and so on.

Source: Principles from Superforecasting: The *Art and Science of Prediction* by Philip Tetlock and Dan Gardner. Table from Phil Simon.

SCORE AND DEPLOY

My NCAA Tournament model described earlier was simple on two levels: First, it didn't require anywhere near the data or statistical techniques required to predict a complex business, economic, or medical outcome. Second, I was testing a discrete event, not an ongoing process. That is, my model had no use beyond March Madness in 1997, although I could have refined it over time.

The vast majority of business models couldn't be more different than my little—albeit effective—Excel spreadsheet. Because these forecasts attempt to describe and predict *ongoing* events of far greater complexity, they need to evolve over time. Customer churn, employee attrition, and credit-card delinquency rates don't end when a team wins a trophy and cuts down the net.

The score-and-deploy phase begins the process of assessing the viability of the model. Questions may well include:

- Is your model working well? How well and how do you really know?
- Are you measuring what you sought to measure?
- Even if you're looking at the right (independent) variables, are their *weights* appropriate?

- How confident are you in your predictions?
- Knowing that you'll never reach complete accuracy, what is an acceptable level of uncertainty?

It's important to note that you might not have access to a pristine and comprehensive dataset to run through your model. At some point, odds are that you will have to decide between including a smaller but cleaner dataset and a larger but impure one. Finally, keep an eye out for tactical and operational issues. If people aren't adhering to your model's recommendations for whatever reason, it will ultimately suffer.

EVALUATE AND IMPROVE

You've developed the first or fifth iteration of your model and want to see if it's describing or predicting what you expected. It's now time to audit your model. At a high level, model updates take one of the following three forms:

1. **Simple data refresh:** In this case, you replace a model's existing dataset with a different one. The new dataset may include newer records, older ones, or a combination of both.
2. **Model update:** This is a complete or partial rebuild. (This may entail new variables and associated weights.)
3. **Combination:** This method fuses the first two. That is, you significantly alter the model *and* run a different dataset through it.

Again, it's hard to promulgate absolute rules here because certain events are much harder to explain—*let alone predict*—than others. A model that explains 20 percent of the variance of a complex issue might exceed expectations, while one that explains 65 percent may be woefully inadequate.

Questions here typically include:

- What data sources are you missing? Which ones are worth including?
- Which data sources may dry up? What will you do if that happens? (It's a mistake to assume that a source will be freely available forever just because this is the case today.)
- Which data sources should you retire?

- Which weights need adjusting? By how much?
- Will your model improve or diminish if you make fundamental changes?
- What are the time implications?
- What happens if you make a big mistake? (A major risk to a company's core product or service is very different than one to some "moonshot.")

I don't know the answers to questions such as these for your organization's specific problems. Regardless of what you're trying to achieve, though, it's imperative to regularly review your models for efficacy. Put differently, disavow yourself of the "set-it-and-forget-it" mind-set. As described in the Introduction (see "Analytics and the Need for Speed"), the world changes faster than ever today. At a bare minimum, complacent companies risk missing big opportunities. In the extreme, they may become obsolete. Before leaving his post as CEO at Cisco Systems, John Chambers gave a keynote speech in which he predicted that 40 percent of today's companies will "not exist in a meaningful way in 10 years."[3]

❷ TIP

After completing the cycle, it's time to repeat it. Ideally, you have developed better questions than you asked the first time and even a few answers.

CHAPTER REVIEW AND DISCUSSION QUESTIONS

- What are the six steps in the framework for Agile analytics?
- Why is it essential to complete every step in the framework?
- Why is business discovery so essential?
- Do models need to be complicated to be effective? Why or why not?
- Are experts particularly adept at making accurate predictions? Why or why not?
- What are the personality characteristics that make for better forecasting?

NEXT

Part Two has covered the essentials of analytics and one specific Agile method: Scrum. It also provided a general framework for performing analytics. It's now time to move from theory to practice.

Part Three details a number of organizations' efforts to make sense of data and deploy analytics. Yes, it's case-study time. As we'll soon see, with analytics, moving from theory to practice is often easier said than done.

NOTES

1. Darrell Rigby, Jeff Sutherland, and Hirotaka Takeuchi, "Embracing Agile," *Harvard Business Review*, May 2016, http://bit.ly/23JbM5k.
2. Alix Spiegel, "So You Think You're Smarter Than a CIA Agent," Parallels, NPR, April 2, 2014, http://n.pr/231BDSa.
3. Julie Bort, "Retiring Cisco CEO Delivers Dire Prediction: 40% of Companies Will Be Dead in 10 Years," Business Insider, June 8, 2015, https://read.bi/1HmHyIU.

PART **THREE**

Analytics in Action

I t's time to show, not tell.

Part Three applies the topics covered so far in the context of a series of case studies. Note that, for several reasons, only the University Tutoring Center case study closely follows the framework discussed in Chapter 6. First, the students adhered to this model under my indirect supervision. Second, I don't possess inside information on how some of the other companies produced their specific analytics. (Firms justifiably are loath to reveal their methods.) It's likely that they didn't formally adhere to this precise scheme. Finally, there is no single correct paradigm for Agile analytics. Remember a few of the Agile principles from Chapter 4:

- Individuals and interactions over processes and tools
- Responding to change over following a plan

This part includes the following chapters:

- **Chapter 7:** University Tutoring Center: An In-Depth Case Study on Agile Analytics
- **Chapter 8:** People Analytics at Google/Alphabet: Not Your Father's HR Department

- **Chapter 9:** The Anti-Google: Beneke Pharmaceuticals
- **Chapter 10:** Ice Station Zebra Medical: How Agile Methods Solved a Messy Health-Care Data Problem
- **Chapter 11:** Racial Profiling at Nextdoor: Using Data to Build a Better App and Combat a PR Disaster

CHAPTER 7

University Tutoring Center

An In-Depth Case Study on Agile Analytics

Make voyages. Attempt them. There's nothing else.

—Tennessee Williams

I n August 2016, I began my new career as a faculty member at the largest public university in Arizona.* I teach full-time in the Department of Information Systems.

By way of background, the university prides itself on inclusion and diversity. In 2015, its president, Dr. Michael Crow, wrote *Designing the New American University*, along with William Dabars. The book outlined

---

*If my motivations intrigue you, see http://bit.ly/2niSggf.

Dr. Crow's bold vision for the future of education in this country. At the risk of bragging, the strategy is paying off, and the university is racking up the accolades. For instance, in March 2017, *U.S. News & World Report* ranked its MBA program number 25 in the world. The 2015 Open Doors Report of the International Educational Exchange ranked it the number-four overall college or university for international students.*

As I learned during my first week at orientation, my new employer offers its students no shortage of resources. Many take advantage of its workshops and seminars, career counselors, and writing and tutoring centers. (For my part, I'm usually not bored during my office hours.)

Although I am relatively new to academia, the charter of the school's tutoring center (known as the University Tutoring Center or the UTC) doesn't seem unique. Most universities' comparable departments face the same primary objective: to provide the most tutoring services in as many subjects as possible during their hours of operations for the lowest cost possible. In other words, tutoring centers are in the optimization business.

THE UTC AND PROJECT BACKGROUND

Starting in 2014, Shannon Bullock began working at the UTC as its student success center coordinator. In her role, Bullock matches supply and demand for undergraduate tutors across a wide variety of subjects: marketing, statistics, economics, accounting, math, finance, and information systems—not to mention a fair number of emerging technologies. Bullock manages a staff of 25 tutors and 11 desk assistants. In any given semester, the UTC assists nearly 10,000 undergraduate students.

As mentioned earlier, Bullock walks a veritable tightrope. Employ too many tutors—*or the wrong types of tutors at the wrong times*—and she is wasting the UTC's limited budget. Employ too few, and students fail

---

* See http://bit.ly/2mBxm7S.

to receive much-needed help, complain, and potentially fail classes and drop out of school.

In making her past staffing decisions, Bullock wasn't exactly throwing darts at a board. By her own admission, though, she wasn't exactly taking an ideal, systematic approach to tackling her optimization problem either. In other words, she wasn't using data and analytics.

In the fall of 2016, Bullock found herself at a crossroads. The status quo was becoming increasingly problematic for several reasons. First, over the past few years the UTC had been expanding at an increasing rate. As a result, many of its best and most popular tutors had started to burn out. They reported feeling overworked, and their performance subsequently decreased.

Second, Bullock's optimization problem involved more than course subjects; the UTC's issue was multidimensional. Even if she could properly staff the UTC with, say, seasoned accounting tutors, there was another factor at play: language. Because of the university's large international contingent, Bullock had to find tutors fluent in Spanish, Chinese, Korean, and a few other languages. Some foreign students simply couldn't communicate effectively with English-speaking tutors.

Last, the UTC faced the very real possibility of significantly increased labor costs in 2017, something that ultimately did happen. In February 2017, Arizona voters approved Proposition 206, a referendum on the minimum wage. As a result, "an estimated 700,000 low-wage workers received an increase to a minimum $10 per hour from $8.05 on January 1, and their wages will increase to $12 an hour in 2020. The measure also requires most employers to provide sick time to their workers."*

Bullock finally decided to turn to data and analytics for solutions. In August of 2016, she engaged a group of five students in my Enterprise Analytics (CIS450) class for a semester-long capstone project. Table 7.1 shows the five undergraduate students who worked with the UTC and their Scrum roles.

---

* Ultimately, Bullock did face higher student labor costs. The new Arizona law specifically exempted college students. For more, see http://bit.ly/2qunj7y.

Table 7.1 Team Composition and Roles

Team Member	Role
Zachary Scott	Product Owner
Sasha Yotter	Scrum Master
Alex Luo	Team Member
Saki Iida	Team Member
Nathan Wall	Team Member

Source: Phil Simon.

PROJECT GOALS AND KICKOFF

Bullock met with her team not long after the semester began and communicated her goals for the project. Everything was on the table, including possibly changing the fundamental way in which the UTC operates. That is, Bullock was open to move from the center's current "open season" (i.e., offering all classes at all times) to a more structured environment. Perhaps the UTC would only offer certain subjects on certain days and at certain times. Bullock wanted the team to create a user-friendly tool that would routinely yield optimized tutoring schedules.

This meant extensive data and analytics.

User Stories

High-level goals and ideas serve as useful starting points. Still, as we've seen, by themselves they don't lend themselves to successful outcomes. In keeping with Scrum, the team conducted interviews with Bullock with the goal of eliciting proper user stories. These conversations ultimately resulted in the product backlog presented in Table 7.2.

Table 7.2 User Stories for Tutoring Project

User Role	User Story	T-Shirt Size	Priority or Release Version	Notes
Tutor	As a tutor, I want to make sure that my workload is fair and I am not overwhelmed.	M	3	Alleviate any bottlenecks.
Student	As a student, I want to make sure that the UTC can tutor in the subject I need.	L	4	

User Role	User Story	T-Shirt Size	Priority or Release Version	Notes
Coordinator	As a tutoring center coordinator, I want to make sure that the UTC is being properly staffed.	L	3	
Coordinator	As a tutoring center coordinator, I want to know when the UTC is busy and why.	S	1	
Coordinator	As a tutoring center coordinator, I want to know any tutoring inefficiencies as soon as possible.	L	4	
Coordinator	As a tutoring center coordinator, I want to know the makeup of the tutees.	L	2	
Coordinator	As a tutoring center coordinator, I want to meet the language needs of international students.	M	2	
Coordinator	As a tutoring center coordinator, I want to foster a relationship with the economics tutoring center.	S	3	
School Administrator	As a school administrator, I want to make sure student information is being handled in compliance with FERPA.*	M	1	Anonymize the data.

Source: Analytics team.

Note that the team converted the T-shirt sizes in Table 7.2 into Fibonacci numbers. Either one works, but as Chapter 5 shows, the latter allows for the easy calculation of sprint velocities and burn-down charts. Table 7.3 demonstrates this.

Table 7.3 Fibonacci Number Conversion Table

T-Shirt Size	Fibonacci Number
Small	3
Medium	5
Large	8

Source: Analytics team.

---

* Family Educational Rights and Privacy Act (FERPA) is a United States federal law that governs the access of educational information and records.

Business and Data Discovery

Before beginning to build its model or tool, the team correctly took a step back. In the parlance of the framework described in Chapter 6, the team performed data discovery.

By way of background, tutors and tutees at the UTC sign in to a simple Google Sheet that tracks student name, student number, time arrived, and subject. Sometimes tutees forgot to swipe in and out of the UTC. As a result, Bullock occasionally failed to collect certain student information. In some instances, she recorded inaccurately long tutoring sessions.

Bullock provided the information on this sheet to the analytics team. Generally speaking, the data was of high quality, although it was certainly not perfect. The team began by identifying the following:

- The UTC's busiest days and times, and then ranking them
- Which tutors taught which subjects on which days

The team performed business data discovery here (see the first two phases of the framework in Figure 6.1). In the words of one of my students, tutor and project Scrum Master Sasha Yotter:

> The first iteration was the most important part of the project. It was all about discovery and learning about the data. What do we have? What patterns do we see? When we went back and evaluated the first iteration, we started seeing the errors with our analysis. Why do the ratios seem to show patterns that don't reflect what it feels like when we're working in the tutoring center?

Note the fundamental questions that Yotter and her teammates asked. Also note how receptive Bullock was to the team's suggestions. (The case study in Chapter 9 reveals how individual receptiveness to analytics isn't necessarily a given.)

With these questions in mind and the data forthcoming, the team had planted the seeds for a great start in making the UTC more efficient. Over the course of the next three months, the team developed an optimal schedule—one that allowed the UTC to serve the maximum number of tutees while staying within its budget. What's more, it would address the increasing problem of tutor burnout.

EMBRACING NEW COLLABORATION TOOLS

The group realized the silliness of relying on e-mail as a collaboration tool today.* The analytics team used Microsoft Excel to build its model, analyze the UTC's data, and create heat maps. For collaboration, the group relied upon Google Drive for document and file sharing. Waffle.io handled the team's user stories.

* The students' professor may have made that point a few times during class.

ITERATION ONE

In the first iteration, the team analyzed UTC for the first four weeks of the fall 2016 semester. To keep its initial batch small, the group intelligently limited its analysis to the UTC's three most popular subjects: accounting (ACC), math (MAT), and information systems (CIS). The team also anonymized tutee information to comply with the U.S. Family Educational Rights and Privacy Act. The team then determined the UTC's busiest times. It created heat maps for each subject, an example of which is displayed in Figure 7.1.

	Monday	Tuesday	Wednesday	Thursday	Friday	Total
9:00 a.m.	2	2	5	5	13	27
10:00 a.m.		6	2	16	17	41
11:00 a.m.		12	7	20	17	56
12:00 p.m.	1	4	11	14	16	46
1:00 p.m.	4	12	16	15	22	69
2:00 p.m.	1	13	7	16	3	40
3:00 p.m.	6	6	6	18		36
4:00 p.m.	2	9	5	7		23
5:00 p.m.	1	1	2	12		16
6:00 p.m.		2		2		4
Total	17	67	61	125	88	358

Figure 7.1 Heat Map for UTC Accounting Tutees
Source: Analytics team.

As Bullock had intuitively sensed, Thursday was the busiest day of the week for students seeking help in accounting. (The data in Figure 7.1 confirmed as much.) The most popular period in which students sought assistance in this subject was 10:00 a.m. to 2:00 p.m. Not surprisingly, few students wanted help here on Monday morning and Friday afternoon. The team repeated the exercise for math, shown in Figure 7.2.

	Monday	Tuesday	Wednesday	Thursday	Friday	Total
9:00 a.m.	1	0	2	4	1	8
10:00 a.m.	2	3	3	3	2	13
11:00 a.m.	1	3	0	1	5	10
12:00 p.m.	1	2	3	3	6	15
1:00 p.m.	1	3	11	8	8	31
2:00 p.m.	0	9	3	1	3	16
3:00 p.m.	2	2	1	4		9
4:00 p.m.	0	7	4	0		11
5:00 p.m.	2	4	3	1		10
6:00 p.m.	1	0	0	1		2
Total	11	33	30	26	25	125

Figure 7.2 Heat Map for UTC Math Tutees
Source: Analytics team.

Although accounting was three times as popular as math, the general tutee trend between the two subjects is similar. Interestingly, CIS received nearly 60 percent of its tutoring requests on Tuesday. Assignments for the required freshman introductory course Computer Application and Information Technology (CIS105) were due that day.

ITERATION TWO

As all good Scrum teams do, the analytics group had produced something meaningful very quickly. Not only had it gained a better understanding of the UTC's most popular subjects, days, and times, but the team also shared its new understanding with Bullock. The group was ready to tackle the next set of user stories on its product backlog.

Specifically, in the second iteration, the team sought to accomplish the following:

- Compare the number of tutees to tutor availability for all subjects.
- Implement a method of tracking which tutors were helping the most students.
- Determine tutees' ethnicities with the ultimate intent of tying this information to tutor language proficiency.
- Gain insights into international students' studying habits.

By using the UTC's data to develop new analytics, the team hoped to unearth specific and nonobvious UTC scheduling inefficiencies. For instance, at what times and dates was it employing too many tutors and/or too few? Aside from discrete shortages or surfeits, the team aimed to discover tutee patterns throughout the week. When was a spate of students likely to come in seeking statistics help? Perhaps the UTC should incorporate those patterns into its tutor-scheduling process. Again, this entailed building heat maps, but this time for tutors—not tutees. Figure 7.3 shows the heat map for accounting *tutors*.

	Monday	Tuesday	Wednesday	Thursday	Friday	Total
9:00 AM	1	1	2	2	2	8
10:00 AM	2	1	3	2	3	11
11:00 AM	2	1	2	2	1.5	8.5
12:00 PM	1	3	2.5	3	1.5	11
1:00 PM	1	2.5	2	2.5	3	11
2:00 PM	1	4	3	2	3	13
3:00 PM	3	4.5	3	2.5		13
4:00 PM	3	3	2.5	2		10.5
5:00 PM	3	1.5	2	2		8.5
6:00 PM	1	1	2	2		6
Total	18	22.5	24	2	14	100.5

Figure 7.3 Heat Map for UTC Accounting Tutors
Source: Analytics team.

By doing this, the team could now easily calculate student-to-tutor ratios (STRs) for each subject, day, and hour. Within a month, Bullock could now view average STRs with unprecedented granularity. Figure 7.4 displays this heat map.

	Monday	Tuesday	Wednesday	Thursday	Friday	Total
9:00 a.m.	2.00	2.00	2.50	2.50	6.50	3.10
10:00 a.m.	0.00	6.00	0.70	8.00	5.70	4.08
11:00 a.m.	0.00	12.00	3.50	10.00	11.30	7.36
12:00 p.m.	1.00	1.30	4.40	4.70	10.70	4.42
1:00 p.m.	4.00	4.80	8.00	6.00	7.30	6.02
2:00 p.m.	1.00	3.30	2.30	8.00	1.00	3.12
3:00 p.m.	2.00	1.30	2.00	7.20		3.13
4:00 p.m.	0.70	3.00	2.00	3.50		2.30
5:00 p.m.	0.30	0.70	1.00	6.00		2.00
6:00 p.m.	0.00	2.00	0.00	1.00		0.75
Average	1.10	3.64	2.64	5.69	7.08	3.63

Figure 7.4 Heat Map for UTC Accounting STRs
Source: Analytics team.

Note that times with values of 0 represent tutors sitting idly without any tutees. (Some of the members of the analytics team worked for Bullock as tutors, and they had occasionally witnessed this phenomenon.) For example, as Figure 7.3 shows, accounting tutors on Monday and Wednesday were on standby waiting for tutees. In this case, accounting tutors were wasting the UTC's money as well as their time. While Bullock may not have been able to avoid this unfortunate scenario altogether, data and analytics could minimize its occurrence.

Analytics Results in a Fundamental Change

The analytics team had already made significant progress. The heat maps from the second iteration provided Bullock with new and valuable insights. In many instances, tutees outnumbered tutors by unhealthy margins. (Figure 7.4 shows how STRs varied wildly by a factor of 40: from 0.3 to 12.0.) At the high end of this range, students did receive the individualized attention they needed. This was problematic, and the team wondered whether adding more tutors in each subject was a viable solution. Perhaps shuffling the deck might prove fruitful.

For instance, the team pondered the following scenario: What if Bullock slotted three accounting tutors on Monday morning, but no students showed up? Down the hall, though, 15 tutees awaited assistance in math. This begged the question: What, if anything, could the UTC do about this mismatch?

As it turns out, the answer was quite a bit.

The team correctly inferred that many tutors could handle multiple subjects during their shifts. Zach did not need to tutor exclusively in accounting in four-hour blocks, especially if he possessed other expertise. He could tutor accounting for 30 minutes, CIS for two hours, and then move back to accounting for another 90 minutes. More generally, Bullock could assign certain tutors to subject A. On the basis of student demand and tutor knowledge, she could then move them to subject B. No, this change wouldn't eradicate tutor idle time, but it would minimize it. The team's next iteration implemented this new strategy.

Moving Beyond Simple Tutor Utilization

Bullock now knew which students needed, and, ultimately, received help by subject, time, and day. Tutors, however, had never entered their individual tutees' names and student IDs after completing their sessions. Tutors just moved to the next tutee in the queue. Because of this, Bullock lacked insight into which tutors helped which students.

The analytics team realized that the UTC could easily capture this data. Indeed, it represented a massive opportunity. On a number of levels, this would allow for far more extensive analytics. For instance, this data would allow Bullock to move beyond knowing each tutor's individual utilization—and trends. Rather, she could then easily determine:

- The UTC's most and least active tutors. (In the case of the former, she may discover which are most susceptible to burnout.)
- The busiest tutors *in each subject*.
- Things such as the most prolific tutors for incoming CIS freshmen.
- Which tutors received the highest rankings from different groups of tutees. The team could cut this data by tutee gender, nationality, and year. (Maybe certain tutors have a knack for explaining relational databases to Asian students.)

To this end, the team added a simple yet critical field to the UTC's existing Google Sheet: tutor name. The team attempted to accomplish this automatically via a pop-up using JavaScript-based Google Apps

Script.* (Because of some technical issues, the team ultimately needed to postpone this addition.)

Meeting International Students' Needs

Because of the university's large international contingent, the analytics team examined tutee ethnicities and international students' most popular subjects and courses. Ideally, this would provide Bullock with insights on precisely when she would need to staff multilingual tutors. Figure 7.5 shows the group's findings.

Course	White	Hispanic/ Latino	International Students	Asian	African American
ACC340	71	17	20	10	0
CIS105	53	32	13	7	8
ACC231	59	18	3	9	12
ACC241	31	10	13	17	1
ECN212	31	13	1	5	3
MAT210	32	17	3	8	3
MAT211	23	11	2	1	2
ECN306	15	6	6	10	0
ECN312	19	3	7	3	3
ECN313	20	8	4	2	0

Figure 7.5 Tutee Ethnicities and Courses Requested
Source: Analytics team.

Equipped with this information, Bullock could easily determine which times and days appealed to each ethnicity. Figure 7.6 displays this view for Hispanic students.

By using simple pivot tables in Microsoft Excel, the team determined the average number of international students by country, day of the week, and time. Because they followed Scrum and the framework outlined in Chapter 6, the team had made real progress, but it wasn't satisfied. Remember that Agile methods build on the successes of the prior iteration.

---

* For more on this, see https://developers.google.com/apps-script.

	CIS105	ACC231	MAT210	TOTAL
9:00 a.m.	1.00		1.00	2.00
10:00 a.m.	1.00	2.00	1.00	4.00
11:00 a.m.	3.00	3.00		6.00
12:00 p.m.	4.00		4.00	8.00
1:00 p.m.	2.00	3.00	2.00	7.00
2:00 p.m.	2.00	5.00	3.00	10.00
3:00 p.m.		1.00	1.00	2.00
4:00 p.m.	6.00	4.00	2.00	12.00
5:00 p.m.	4.00		3.00	7.00
6:00 p.m.	9.00			9.00
Total	32.00	18.00	17.00	67.00

Figure 7.6 Hispanic Tutees' Popular Subjects and Visit Hours
Source: Analytics team.

ITERATION THREE

In the third iteration, the analytics team created a user-friendly, Excel-based tool that Bullock could use to make future scheduling decisions. The model relied on previous tutee data, specifically tutee swipe-in data. (Students use their ID cards for this purpose, among others.)

By incorporating this information into its model, the team improved STR accuracy. It had now accounted for each tutor's utilization, something that the UTC had never done before. For instance, if Sasha tutored both math and statistics in a shift, then she should count as only 0.5 of a tutor in both subjects. Counting her as 1.0 in each overstates her utilization. Figure 7.7 represents this new schedule.

As Figure 7.7 shows, the team fundamentally changed how the UTC counted tutors. Originally, if Zach tutored in both math and accounting, then he counted as one full tutor for both subjects. However, if Jesse needed help for math and Walter needed accounting assistance, Zach

	CIS	MAT	ACC	FIN	ECN
9:00 AM - 9:30 AM	1.00	0.00	1.00	0.50	0.50
9:30 AM - 10:00 AM	1.00	0.00	1.00	0.50	0.50
10:00 AM - 10:30 AM	1.50	0.00	1.00	0.50	1.00
10:30 AM - 11:00 AM	1.50	0.00	1.00	0.50	1.00
11:00 AM - 11:30 AM	1.50	0.50	1.00	0.50	0.50
11:30 AM - 12:00 PM	2.00	0.50	0.50	0.00	1.00
12:00 PM - 12:30 PM	1.00	1.33	1.33	0.33	1.00
12:30 PM - 1:00 PM	1.00	1.33	1.33	0.33	1.00
1:00 PM - 1:30 PM	1.00	0.83	0.83	0.33	1.00
1:30 PM - 2:00 PM	2.00	0.50	0.50	0.00	2.50
2:00 PM - 2:30 PM	2.00	1.00	1.00	0.00	2.50
2:30 PM - 3:00 PM	2.00	1.00	1.00	0.00	2.00

Figure 7.7 Representation of New Tutor Schedule
Source: Analytics team.

could not concurrently help both students. To fix this, the team counted tutors as 0.5 for math and 0.5 for accounting. (Three would count as 0.33, etc.) This allowed the UTC to more accurately gauge tutor utilization.

ITERATION FOUR

Based on the progress from iteration three, Bullock changed the tutor schedule and began using the team's new STRs. Although tutors *can* teach more than one subject in a shift, most found this mentally draining. For instance, Victor is slotted to tutor accounting from noon to 1:00 p.m. and then switch to CIS. Earvin walks into the UTC at 12:55 p.m. and needs help in accounting. Victor is the next tutor up, but can only tutor Earvin for five minutes. Both tutors and tutees struggled with the frequent shift changes. "We assigned single subjects to tutors for the entire semester," says tutor and product owner Zach Scott. "This eliminated the switching costs of tutoring multiple subjects."

For the final iteration, the team examined the UTC's schedule changes and their results. Was it now operating more efficiently than before the project began? The answer was a clear yes: the new STRs were significantly lower. For instance, as Figure 7.8 illustrates, the accounting STR on Thursday dropped 53 percent (from 4.12 to 1.94).

Accounting	Old ACC Ratio	New ACC Ratio
9:00 a.m. – 9:30 a.m.	1.86	1.50
9:30 a.m. – 10:00 a.m.	1.86	1.50
10:00 a.m. – 10:30 a.m.	4.86	2.75
10:30 a.m. – 11:00 a.m.	4.86	2.75
11:00 a.m. – 11:30 a.m.	4.29	1.38
11:30 a.m. – 12:00 p.m.	8.57	2.75
12:00 p.m. – 12:30 p.m.	3.22	0.88
12:30 p.m. – 1:00 p.m.	2.26	0.88
1:00 p.m. – 1:30 p.m.	3.61	0.75
1:30 p.m. – 2:00 p.m.	8.00	0.00
2:00 p.m. – 2:30 p.m.	4.00	4.00
2:30 p.m. – 3:00 p.m.	4.00	4.00
3:00 p.m. – 3:30 p.m.	3.01	2.00
3:30 p.m. – 4:00 p.m.	3.22	2.00
Average	4.12	1.94

Figure 7.8 Accounting STR, Thursday: Old versus New
Source: Analytics team.

In ending the project, the team also made recommendations for future semesters based on its most recent findings.

RESULTS

Over the course of a single semester, Bullock garnered a far better understanding of the skills of her tutors, the needs of the university's undergraduate students, and how data and analytics can fuse the two.

Bullock allowed the team to make changes to the UTC's scheduling system after each release. As such, the team was able to analyze the effectiveness of its changes. The ability to do this in small batches was both invaluable and very much in keeping with Agile analytics.

Compared with its antecedent, the UTC's new tutor schedule has drastically reduced tutor frustration. This is especially true with accounting tutors. Bullock can now determine which tutees come in most frequently and possible red flags. Perhaps frequent student visits correlate with undesirable outcomes such as poor grades, academic probation, and even withdrawal.

LESSONS

This case study proves that significant results via analytics need not take years, cutting-edge software, and a team of pricey consultants. In this instance, it only took an open mind-set, Microsoft Excel, quality data, and a group of intelligent, curious students following a superior method. Put these together, and you can achieve amazing things in a very short period of time.

CHAPTER REVIEW AND DISCUSSION QUESTIONS

- What problem was the analytics team attempting to solve?
- In what ways did the team benefit from gathering user stories at the beginning of the project?
- Did the team need to overcome data-quality issues? Why was this important?
- What did the team release in its first iteration?
- How did the team use feedback to improve its model in each iteration?
- Was the project ultimately successful? Why or why not?

NEXT

The next case study examines the use of analytics on a much larger scale and in a much larger organization. I'm betting that you've heard of this company, but probably not in this particular context.

CHAPTER 8

People Analytics at Google/Alphabet

Not Your Father's HR Department

Without data, you're just another person with an opinion.

—W. Edwards Deming

We all have our own views on the way that our organization, department, and teams ought to handle things. I suspect that most of us think that, if given the chance, we would do a better job than our bosses do. *Things would be different if I were running things.* But would they really, and, more important, how would you know?

THE VALUE OF BUSINESS EXPERIMENTS

When many people think of proper experiments, they envision scientists in white coats lurking over participants (usually college kids) paid $10 per hour. Maybe Stanley Milgram's faux electric shocks come to mind. Few people think of experiments in a business context, and that's unfortunate. As we see in this chapter, experiments often serve as valuable ways of conclusively determining if ideas, products, and policies actually work—and if they work better than alternatives.

Much to the chagrin of animal rights' groups, pharmaceutical companies try different combinations of compounds on lab rats to test the efficacy of drugs under development. (Better on mice than on humans, I suppose.) And it doesn't stop there. For instance, CapitalOne routinely mails thousands of credit card offers with slightly different terms, including:

- Annual percentage rate (APRs)
- Credit limits
- Cash-advance fees
- Perks, such as bonus miles

Employees at CapitalOne—one of my former employers—are not doing this because they are bored. They know that different types of people respond differently to different offers, but they don't know the right combination of terms. Consider two simple propositions:

- **Offer A:** An offer for a card with a 13 percent APR and a $5,000 credit limit generates a 3.2 percent response rate.
- **Offer B:** An offer for a card with a 15 percent APR and a $3,000 credit limit generates only a 2.2 percent response rate.

Although a 1 percent difference in response rate might not seem like much, it is—especially when tens of thousands of people receive these offers. The data *proves* that consumers respond more to Offer A than to Offer B. Beyond different numbers (rates, APRs, and the like), CapitalOne experiments with the colors, fonts, and imagery on its envelopes. (Yes, they matter as well.)

CapitalOne has been doing this for years, and, to be fair, so has just about every credit card company. But the notion that experiments only work on prospective *customers* in one industry simply isn't true. One prominent company has been doing it for years on its *employees* and its results illustrate the remarkable power of data and analytics—if you're willing to embrace them.

PILAB'S ADVENTURES IN ANALYTICS

At some point, you may have heard of X, Google's famous "moonshot" division.* X is responsible for a range of oddball ideas, including:

- **Glass:** The much-maligned, augmented-reality headset[†]
- **Google Contact Lens**
- **Body Authentication and Vault:** A password killer
- **Calico:** The life extension project[‡]

You read right. At one point, the company, formerly known as *Google*, was working on curing death. At least Larry and Sergey aren't lacking ambition. X has killed more than 100 far-fetched projects that didn't show sufficient signs of bearing fruit.[§]

Perhaps the most fascinating group within Google, though, falls under people operations, or POPS, the company's name for *human resources (HR)*. Up until recently, Brian Welle reported directly to Laszlo Bock, the company's senior vice president of people operations. (In May of 2017, Recode reported that Bock is launching a data- and tech-based people analytics start-up called Humu.)

PiLab hires social scientists to specifically study Google and identify areas for improvement. Writing for *Slate*, Farhad Manjoo described how PiLab gathers and analyzes data to ask and answer fundamental questions such as:

> How often should you remind people to contribute to their 401(k)s, and what tone should you use? And say you

---

* X now falls under the umbrella of Google's parent company, Alphabet.
† Here's my early and (I hope) humorous review of it: http://bit.ly/2mZwA8n.
‡ In August of 2015, Google folded Calico into its new parent company Alphabet.
§ For more about this, see http://read.bi/2mHbrO7.

want to give someone a raise—how should you do it in a way that maximizes his happiness? Should you give him a cash bonus? Stock? A raise? More time off?[1]

Lest you think that these are theoretical thought experiments à la Schrödinger's cat, think again. The answers solve real problems. For instance, in 2010, companies began poaching Google employees at an increasing rate. Facebook was particularly aggressive. In response, PiLab posed the following question to Google employees: Would you rather receive a $1,000 annual raise or $2,000 as a bonus?

By and large, PiLab learned that Googlers valued base pay above everything else. "When we offered a bonus of X, they valued that at what it costs us. But if you give [people] a dollar in base pay, they value it at more than a dollar because of the long-term certainty," said Prasad Setty, now vice president of people analytics and compensation. Not surprisingly, the program worked. Along with a 10 percent raise,* Google lowered attrition to its rivals.

Communication

PiLab's curiosity isn't easily sated. Nothing seems off limits; it appears to have carte blanche to investigate whatever it likes. Case in point: As I wrote in *Message Not Received*, the average employee today receives roughly 120 to 150 e-mails per day, but how many of them are really valuable? And do those messages ultimately do anything beyond annoy employees who already have too much on their plates? Again, PiLab used data to answer that question:

> In one experiment, the people analytics team found that sending managers an e-mail just before they met a new employee to remind them of a simple agenda for the first four days of employment boosted that employee's productivity by between 5 percent and 14 percent.[2]

---

* Read the internal memo announcing it here: http://read.bi/2mNxmVr.

PiLab doesn't just ask these types of questions and move on, nor is it content with merely finding the answer. In keeping with Google culture, PiLab uses the data to effect policy changes.

A BETTER APPROACH TO HIRING

For most of its first decade, Google had justifiably earned a reputation as a tough place to land a job. This stemmed from several factors. For one, its two iconic founders were über-smart engineers. To put it very kindly, at first they didn't appreciate more traditional business functions such as management and marketing.*

Douglas Edwards wrote about his struggles as Google's first marketing hire in *I'm Feeling Lucky: The Confessions of Google Employee Number 59*. In 1999, he joined the company and quickly butted heads with his superiors. They weren't convinced that marketing actually mattered; to them, he was just a guy who couldn't code. At one point, Edwards pitched his bosses on a $1 million marketing campaign. Unimpressed, they asked him to *prove* that the company shouldn't just give the same amount of money to a country in need.

Beyond a historical hostility to nonengineers, the company's legendary interview questions aren't exactly for the faint of heart. Forget softies such as "Where do you see yourself in five years?" or "Do you have any weaknesses?" Expect standard behavior-based interview questions at Google to be sprinkled with doozies such as the following:

- Design an evacuation plan for the building.
- Estimate the number of tennis balls that can fit into a plane.
- How many cars travel across a bridge each day?†

The point of these mind-bending and now infamous queries isn't to obtain a "correct" answer. Rather, Googlers want to know how potential hires *really* think. Are they comfortable with uncertainty? Are they really quantitative or do they just claim to be?

---

* Remember that Google's search engine grew organically (read: without the help of any paid advertising).

† For more, see http://on.inc.com/1MnpGlA.

BETTER RECRUITING VIA TRANSPARENCY

Many prominent companies keep the inner workings of their hiring processes secret. Not Google, a company that reportedly rejects far more than 99 percent of applicants.[3] Scanning resumes can only do so much. Because of this fundamental imbalance between supply and demand, recruiters have to find ways to weed out applicants who lack the skills that Google covets. To be sure, it's a good problem to have, but it is a problem nevertheless. Two simple solutions have proven effective: transparency in communication and truth in advertising.

Sujay Maheshwari in *Business Insider* detailed an actual e-mail that Google recruiters sent applicants for product manager (PM) positions. Here's an excerpt:

> Google PMs are fluent with numbers. They define the right metrics. They can interpret and make decisions from A/B test results. They don't mind getting their hands dirty. Sometimes they write SQL* queries; other times, they run scripts to extract data from logs. They make their point by crisply communicating their analysis. Some examples of analytical questions:
>
> ■ How many queries per second does Gmail get?
>
> ■ How many iPhones are sold in the United States each year?
>
> ■ As the PM for Google Glass "Enterprise Edition," which metrics would you track? How do you know if the product is successful?[4]

* SQL stands for Structured Query Language.

Eliminating GPA as a Criterion for Hiring

Many heads of HR and recruiters take grade point average (GPA) as gospel. The rationale is straightforward: good grades always indicate a strong work ethic. Still, does the relationship between the two variables *always* hold water?

While at Google, Bock challenged the orthodoxy by hiring people who lacked high GPAs, college degrees, and pristine test scores. In effect, he was asking better, *objectively testable* questions such as:

■ Is a traditional pedigree required to be successful at Google?

■ Is there a relationship between GPA and job performance?

■ Are the answers to these questions universal or do they vary across countries?

His results were astounding. Many of Google's untraditional hires turned out to be quite successful. In a 2013 interview for the *New York Times*, Bock concluded that "GPAs are worthless as a criteria for hiring, and test scores are worthless."[5]

Bock expanded on this notion in his bestselling 2015 book, *Work Rules!: Insights from Inside Google That Will Transform How You Live and Lead*. Applying a universal approach to recruiting was silly. Consider the mind-set of Japanese students:

> When evaluating college students, GPA might seem like a fairly important factor to consider. Not so for candidates in Japan. In Japan, college admissions are largely based on national test results, so high school students focus intensely on doing well on those tests, often attending *juku* (special after-school classes) for 15 to 20 hours each week for years. But once admitted to a premier university, Japanese students don't focus on grades at all. Historically, they enjoy a last gasp of play and freedom between the crush of the *juku* and the monotony of the career of a *sarariman* ("salaryman"—the nomenclature for the expected rule-following, slow, tenure-based progression that characterized Japanese careers in the past). Japanese college grades are virtually useless as a hiring signal, but knowing which college someone attended is helpful, at least for hiring new graduates.

If Google's HR chief approaches analytics in this way, imagine what its engineers and salespeople do. No wonder the company has been so successful. It is willing to zig when others zag.

Using Analytics to Streamline the Hiring Process

Around the turn of the century, Google's interview process had become downright lethargic. It wasn't uncommon for potential hires to gab with a dozen or more current Google employees before receiving an offer letter. Applicants often took to social media and wrote blog posts expressing their dissatisfaction with the company's exhausting hiring process.*

---

* Check out a thread on Hacker News here: http://bit.ly/2mXXfCx.

Beginning in 2006, Google's management began addressing the problem the only way that it knew how: through data. As Tim Fernholz wrote for Quartz:

> The company began Vox Pop, a survey of everyone who came in for an interview, asking them to rate their experience. After assessing the results of hiring decisions and the experience of candidates, the company concluded that four interviews was enough to gain a reliable prediction of whether they'd be a good hire; more than that made little appreciable difference. Google employees now spend less time doing interviews.[6]

This is old hat at Google. As we will see next, the company routinely uses survey data to evaluate and improve a broken business process.

STAFFING

Firms have been surveying their employees for decades. As someone who cut his teeth in HR, I know that many workers often don't take surveys seriously for all sorts of reasons. Sure, some employees are too busy, but many of them believe that nothing substantive will ever come from their responses, so why even bother?

Not at Google. Its Googlegeist survey routinely sports a participation rate of 90 percent because the company actually acts on the results. In the past, Google has used Googlegeist data in all sorts of interesting ways. Put differently, countless HR heads have asked many of the following questions (Google, on the other hand, has definitively answered them):

- Do successful middle managers have certain skills in common— and can you teach those skills to unsuccessful managers? (Answer: yes.)
- Do managers even matter? (Answer: yes. Managers' performance correlates strongly with their employees' performance as well as their likelihood of leaving.)
- Can you organize a company without surveys? (Answer: no, especially one at Google's size.)

Critically, Google provided struggling managers with timely feedback and training. In some cases, problems unearthed on surveys have resulted in managers moving to nonmanagerial roles. This intimate knowledge of what works and why doesn't just help reassigning employees whose skills don't match those required by their current roles. It also helps staffing teams properly.

MATCHING TEAM SKILLS AND NEEDS

Let's say that you have an idea for a new project or product at your company. The specific idea itself doesn't matter here. For the sake of argument, it is an entirely new type of widget that isn't on the market.

Sure, you could quit your current job and launch your own start-up, but you know that most new enterprises fail. Beyond that, you actually like your job and you aren't in a financial position to incur massive risk at the moment. Still, that idea keeps gnawing at you.

You go to your manager and make your case. She's on board, but she needs to clear it with her own boss. She gets back to you with good news. You can devote three months to the new idea in a vacuum while you continue to meet most of your current responsibilities. You know that your new widget is far more than a one-person endeavor, but you reason that the agreement is better than nothing. If it shows promise, then perhaps more resources will come your way—at least that's what you hope.

Now, let's say that you work at Google. As this chapter shows, a much different scenario awaits you. You pitch your boss the same idea and she loves it. She immediately involves HR—not to file paperwork, but to start the process of staffing your team. Oddly, HR wants plenty of details. It wants to know exactly what your widget will entail. In other words, *HR wants data.*

Are people in the department just being nosy? Hardly. HR needs this information because it isn't interested in merely finding employees who are either "on the bench" or would like a transfer to different departments. Rather, HR will try to find *the right employees* to maximize the chance that your new product is successful—and not just in terms of programming

(Continued)

skills. HR wants your team to consist of the right number of people, the right personality types, and the right balance of men and women. And it doesn't stop there:

- Where should the team actually work?
- Are its members collocated or do they work remotely?
- When should that change, if at all?

I'll bet that you have never encountered a single HR professional who asks questions like that, never mind an entire department that does. Remarkably, this is the way that Google sees HR: neither as an administrative apparatus nor as the company's internal police. At Google, the vast majority of people decisions are based on data and analytics. In other words, like your boss, HR wants you to be successful and will provide the specific human resources to try to make that happen.

THE VALUE OF PERKS

Google famously provides a number of complimentary benefits to its employees: free dry-cleaning, Wi-Fi-enabled transportation, and massages are the norm. To be sure, these result in great PR, but in theory, some of them might do more harm than good.

Consider the company's free gourmet food. Might it contribute to a "plumper" workforce? Could this, in turn, ultimately cause Google's health insurance costs to skyrocket?

It's a valid question—and one that PiLab wasn't afraid to ask. Why not test the size of plates at the cafeteria? Even Bluto from *Animal House* could only fit so much food on a single plate. Why not put out small dishes along with larger ones?

Google stocked its cafeterias with 8-inch plates alongside 12-inch ones. The smaller ones encouraged people to eat more modest, healthier portions. Oddly,"nobody used the smaller plates until the team explained the goal."[7]

While we're on the subject of food, in 2012, Google famously deserted dessert. As Cliff Kuang of *Fast Company* wrote:

> No longer are M&Ms in clear hanging dispensers. If you're in Google's New York office, you now have to reach into opaque bins. The grab takes effort; the obscuring vessel quells enticement. The switch led to a 9 percent drop in caloric intake from candy in just one week.[8]

Yes, Google quantified the impact. Would you expect anything else?

Innovation on the Lunch Line

The food experiments didn't stop there. As Clayton Christensen manifested in *The Innovator's Dilemma*, large, successful organizations often struggle to sustain innovation. They become complacent, victims of their own success. This is why Blockbuster, Kodak, and so many other ex-titans of industry have fallen and can't get up.

To combat this grim reality, some companies are attempting to induce what Zappos CEO Tony Hsieh calls *collisions*. For the same reason, Apple designed its future headquarters in Cupertino, California, to be a giant circle. In theory, good things can happen when people from different departments informally congregate. In his 2004 book *The Medici Effect*, Frans Johansson argued that random intersections and diversity of thought have led to many important innovations that stretch well beyond the business world.

How could Google encourage similar types of serendipitous interactions among employees? Sure, the company could opt for the usual, hackneyed suspects such as team-bonding exercises and weekend retreats, but PiLab developed a more prosaic solution. How about fostering collisions among employees as they are waiting for free lunch or dinner?

> Dan Cobley, the search giant's UK managing director, told a conference of business leaders at the Albert Hall in London this week that Google's mealtime lines are *intentionally* kept long "because we know people will chat while they're waiting. Chats become ideas, and ideas become projects."[9] [Emphasis mine.]

Of course, it doesn't take long for hungry employees to become cranky employees. To this end, Google reportedly restricts its food queues to three to four minutes.

❓TIP

Google knows the percentage of its promotions that were effective, and, just as important, why. Does HR at your company know this?

Family Leave

At this point, it should be no surprise that Google approaches every problem as a business one. Nothing is exempt from evidence, data, and analytics—and that includes HR and everything under its umbrella.

Passed on August 5, 1993, the U.S. Family and Medical Leave Act (FMLA) mandates that employers must provide certain employees with up to 12 weeks of *unpaid*, job-protected leave per year. Not all employees qualify; they must meet certain thresholds for hours worked in a given timeframe.

Lest you find this excessively generous, FMLA leave is paltry by international standards. Governments in most industrialized countries are far more benevolent. For instance, in Canada, families with newborns can expect nearly one year of at least "partial ongoing income."*

FMLA mandates *minimum* benefits for qualified employees, not *maximum* ones. In the past few years, tech companies in particular have markedly upped their family-leave programs. In February 2017, Facebook COO Sheryl Sandberg announced that the company now offered "four months of paid leave for new parents, moms and dads alike."[10] The social network joined Netflix and Microsoft (among others) in this regard. The goal: to lure the best new employees and retain their existing ones.

Google understood the importance of enhanced maternity leave long before its peers did. In 2007, the company increased its paid time off to 18 weeks from 12. Great PR? Sure, but did the move result in

* For more, see https://tgam.ca/1OwDR6m.

a quantifiable business benefit, and if so, what was it? Google halved the rate at which new mothers quit. YouTube CEO and mother of five Susan Wojcicki wasn't exactly shy about sharing this statistic (see Figure 8.1).

Figure 8.1 Tweet from @SusanWojcicki
Source: Twitter.

Best of all, the program essentially pays for itself. Bock says that if you factor in the recruitment savings, granting mothers five months of leave doesn't cost Google a dime.

RESULTS AND LESSONS

It's impossible to ascertain the precise impact at Google. It is fair to say, however, that HR positively affects the organization on a number of levels. As this chapter shows, at a bare minimum, HR's decisions have helped the company maintain top performers, reduce employee turnover, identify and address real management issues, and hire better. How many CEOs can honestly say that about their HR departments?

Many HR departments struggle with basic blocking and tackling. They parse through headcount numbers trying to determine promotion rates. Google goes way beyond that. Its data-based people management represents a significant part of its long-term success.

To quote from *Tin Cup*, "Greatness courts failure." Maybe PiLab was making a huge mistake by disregarding applicant GPA. Google would know this relatively quickly, not after two years of hiring suboptimal candidates. Thus, by minimizing the time between conception and launch, Agile methods expedited the learning process. As an added benefit, this makes the company more capital- and resource-efficient.

Google proves that analytics is a constant endeavor, not a one-time exercise. As this chapter illustrates, the goal isn't to replace human decision making with data and algorithms; it's to complement intuition with evidence.

CHAPTER REVIEW AND DISCUSSION QUESTIONS

- Why have most companies relied on GPA when making hiring decisions? Why might that not correlate with future performance?
- How does Google treat HR? How is it different than its contemporaries?
- Why did Google increase employee leave? What did the numbers ultimately say about the move?
- Which of PiLab's findings did you find most interesting? Why?
- What other issues should PiLab investigate? Why?

NEXT

The next case study looks at a very different type of HR department and how it refuses to deal with data, much less analytics.

NOTES

1. Farhad Manjoo, "How Google Became Such a Great Place to Work," *Slate*, January 21, 2013, http://slate.me/1GWy4Dn.
2. Tim Fernholz, "Inside Google's Culture of Relentless Self-Surveying," *Quartz*, June 26, 2013, http://bit.ly/2n5JzpB.
3. Chad Catacchio, "One Half of One Percent of Google Applicants Get Hired—Here's How It Works," The Next Web, September 14, 2010, http://bit.ly/2nwFcni.

4. Sujay Maheshwari, "Read the Email a Google Recruiter Sent a Job Candidate to Prepare Him for the Interview," *Business Insider*, March 23, 2017, http://read .bi/2nNvvBz.

5. Adam Bryant, "In Head-Hunting, Big Data May Not Be Such a Big Deal," *New York Times*, June 19, 2013, http://tinyurl.com/hml9nc7.

6. Fernholz, "Inside Google's Culture.".

7. Ibid.

8. Cliff Kuang, "6 Ways Google Hacks Its Cafeterias So Googlers Eat Healthier," *Fast Company*, March 26, 2012, http://bit.ly/2nlJgrj.

9. Tim Walker, "Perks for Employees and How Google Changed the Way We Work (while Waiting in Line)," *The Independent*, September 20, 2013, http://ind .pn/1csYwYN.

10. Taylor Hatmaker, "Facebook Announces Paid Family Sick Leave and New Bereavement Benefits for Employees," *TechCrunch*, February 7, 2017, http://tcrn.ch/2kQZg2d.

CHAPTER **9**

The Anti-Google
Beneke Pharmaceuticals

Where there is power, there is resistance.

—Michel Foucault

At the other end of the analytics spectrum from Google, consider a large drug maker that employed me at the end of the century. I won't name it here, but you can view my LinkedIn profile if you must know. I call it *Beneke Pharmaceuticals* in this chapter; I also changed the names of all of the people who worked with me at the company.

At Beneke, I split my time between its HR and IT departments. Half of my responsibilities entailed supporting a global PeopleSoft implementation. To this end, I traveled to Latin America quite a bit. When not working on this project, I worked in more traditional HR capacities such as compensation and recruiting.

PROJECT BACKGROUND

About midway through my tenure at Beneke, my friend and colleague Lori swung by my cubicle and asked for my help. As someone with a traditional HR background, she was, by her own admission, "numerically challenged." This normally didn't concern her, but things had suddenly changed. Her manager, the fortyish head of college recruiting whom we'll call *Tom*, had given her a very quantitative project. Tom asked Lori to evaluate Beneke's MBA recruiting efforts. Specifically, he wanted answers to the following questions:

- From which colleges and universities was Beneke getting its highest performers?
- Was Beneke best served by recruiting MBAs at Ivy League schools or state universities—in particular, Rutgers?*
- Did graduates at Harvard, Dartmouth, and Yale justify their salary premiums (relative to graduates from state universities)?
- Was Beneke's recruiting department getting the biggest bang for its buck?

Lori didn't know where to begin. She was in luck, though, because I did and I had the time. Fundamentally, this was a data problem. Based on my background, I had the tech and data chops to attack it. In hindsight, I followed a framework remarkably similar to the one described in Chapter 6:

1. Perform business discovery
2. Perform data discovery
3. Prepare the data
4. Model the data

---

* Rutgers is the State University of New Jersey.

5. Score and deploy

6. Evaluate and improve

7. Repeat

Or at least I tried. As you'll soon discover, it's impossible for people to see and hear your message if they close their eyes and cover their ears.

BUSINESS AND DATA DISCOVERY

To begin, I gathered information on recent MBA hires from Beneke's different HR information systems (HRIS). Yes, the company used more than one. As a result, data quality was a chronic thorn in my side throughout my employment there.

I attempted to answer the following questions:

- How long did new hires stay at Beneke?
- How often were they were promoted?
- What were their performance ratings?
- Did new MBAs do better and last longer in different departments (finance, marketing, sales, etc.)?
- Were there appreciable performance differences between MBA hires from different schools? If so, then why?
- Why did MBAs ultimately leave Beneke? Did the company ultimately realize any return on investment?

My questions didn't stop there. Beneke didn't bat a thousand with employment offers. How many companies do? Desirable MBA students generally weren't lacking for offers. Many signed up to work at different firms. Still, what *percentage* of Beneke's offers did MBA candidates accept each year? How did this number vary by university? And what was the direction of this trend? Why were these folks saying no to Beneke? How could the company improve its conversion rate?

I scraped together as much data on formal candidate offers as I could, including base salary, signing bonus, moving expenses, and other incidentals. Finally, I had Lori ask Tom to provide detailed data

that Beneke failed to store in its HR systems. I was particularly interested in the following:

- Tom's team's recruiting expenses (hotel, flight, food, taxi, regis-
  tration fees for job fairs, and the like)
- The number of candidates Beneke interviewed at each school
  (If I had my druthers, I'd also get each candidate's gender, eth-
  nicity, and major as well.)
- The number of candidates Tom and his team brought back to
  Beneke headquarters and all of their related expenses

Equipped with all of this information, I would be able to fully
answer Tom's questions and fully evaluate the state of Beneke's current MBA recruiting efforts. (Ideally, Tom would have also provided his
teams' salaries. I suspected, however, that this information wouldn't
be forthcoming, especially at first. I used estimates that he could easily
replace with real numbers if he liked.)

THE FRICTION BEGINS

Tom did not take too kindly to my requests for information on his
team's recruiting trips. Why was I asking for this data? Through Lori,
he indicated that he was too busy to locate it. (I found this odd, since
his administrative assistant could have quickly sent this to me.)

I started to wonder if Tom really wanted the true answers to his
high-level question, let alone all of mine, after all. Maybe he had asked
Lori to work on the MBA project not in spite of her paucity of analytics experience, *but precisely because of it*. That is, perhaps Tom suspected
all along that her approach wouldn't be particularly quantitative and
analytics-oriented.

Undeterred, I kept going. I didn't know if Tom was truly curious to
see how Beneke was spending its recruiting budget, but by now I certainly was. I built a simple model and made explicit assumptions where
I lacked hard data. This wasn't difficult. Even back then, the nascent
Web made it easy to approximate how much plane tickets, hotel
rooms, transportation, and meals would have cost Tom and his team on
each trip. Coupled with the information that I was able to glean from
Beneke's HRIS, I completed the first round of my model and analysis.

ASTONISHING RESULTS

My results astonished me, so I double-checked all of my numbers and calculations. After all, I was relatively new at Beneke, I was no recruiting expert, and I didn't want to embarrass myself in front of someone senior to me. Part of me wanted to find a major mistake, but alas, my model and its assumptions were sound.

Put simply, Beneke's recent MBA recruiting efforts were far from ideal. Specifically, factoring in base salary, relocation expenses, and recruiting costs, the company was paying more than $150,000 to land each Ivy League MBA in 1999 dollars. I wondered whether this atmospheric number actually made sense. Did Beneke routinely find at these schools its future leaders and high-potential employees who rapidly climbed the executive ranks? I wasn't sure, so I dug deeper into the data. Not so. Ivy Leaguers usually quit after about 18 months at Beneke. Only a handful of these prized hires lasted beyond three years.

The data was unmistakably on one side of the aisle. It was now time to look at the other side. What about newly minted Rutgers grads?

Here, the data told a much different story: Rachel from Rutgers and her cohort appeared to be a veritable bargain for Beneke. Hugo from Harvard earned $105,000 in base salary in his first year. Rachel's compensation equated to a mere $61,000. I did some basic salary forecasting and discovered that it would take more than eight years for Rachel to earn what Hugo did in year one.* By that point, Rachel would presumably be an experienced Beneke employee with solid performance ratings *if she stayed that long.*

But did she? I ran the numbers and discovered clear differences in employee tenure between the cohorts. On average, as Figure 9.1 shows, Rachel worked at Beneke more than four times longer than Hugo did.

All other things being equal, employees who stay with a company longer are more likely to move up the corporate ladder. Not surprisingly, as Figure 9.2 shows, Rutgers hires were six times more likely to be promoted compared to the Ivy League average.

---

* This isn't a gender issue. It all stemmed from initial starting salary differences.

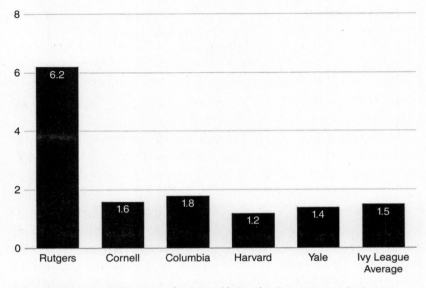

Figure 9.1 Average MBA Years of Tenure with Beneke: Rutgers versus Ivy League Schools
Source: Phil Simon.

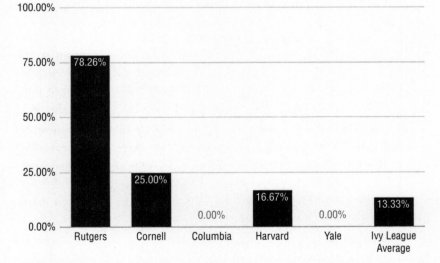

Figure 9.2 Percentage of MBAs Promoted within Three Years at Beneke: Rutgers versus Ivy League Schools
Source: Phil Simon.

Rutgers graduates not only allowed Beneke to save considerably on base salary, but they also stabilized Beneke's workforce.

DEVELOPING OPTIONS

Before reaching any final conclusions, I asked myself one more big question: What if these expensive, short-term Ivy Leaguer rentals still justified their outsize salaries and recruiting costs? No, elite MBAs don't work in the lab and create blockbuster drugs, but what if they sold far more pharmaceuticals than their peers or developed highly effective marketing campaigns?

I would have welcomed a discussion around individual candidates and their specific contributions to the company during their tenures. As far as I could tell, though, none of this was happening. Beneke appeared to be wasting its money with its current MBA recruiting efforts. Absent some revelation, the evidence could not have been clearer. Even if my assumptions on travel expenses and employee contributions were off by a factor of two, it wasn't even a close call.

This begged the question: Since the status quo was clearly untenable, what should the company do about it? Preparing for the inevitable presentation and subsequent discussion, I thought of several options:

- **Option A:** Beneke should immediately cease recruiting at Ivy League schools and pull existing offers. In the future, Beneke should recruit exclusively at Rutgers and other state schools. The juice from the Ivy League didn't remotely justify the squeeze.

- **Option B:** If Ivy League hires truly represented the company's future leaders, then Beneke needed to step up its retention efforts. Getting these folks through the front door meant nothing if they only stayed for a little more than a year. Perhaps these new employees ought to do rotations in cross-functional programs such as finance, sales, and marketing.

Maybe there were more alternatives that didn't occur to me. I was prepared to discuss these options with Tom and his recruiting team. In hindsight, it was time for us to enter the evaluate and improve phase of the framework discussed in Chapter 6.

THE GRAND FINALE

Lori and I presented these findings to Tom. Sadly, his overall demeanor wasn't positive. My overall approach and specific findings clearly made him uncomfortable. Not long after we concluded, Tom confirmed my earlier suspicions about the purity of his quest with a single sentence: "But I *like* recruiting at Ivy League schools."

I'm sure that you do, I thought, but that's not the point. Whether you enjoy visiting Harvard and Cornell and schmoozing with faculty, staff, and students is immaterial. That doesn't matter nearly as much as whether you should be going there in the first place.* Moreover, why did you ask for recruiting analytics if you're just going to ignore them?

Like many of his peers, Tom thought of himself as an HR professional who happened to work in a business, not a businessperson who happened to work in HR. (Chapter 8 demonstrates that there's a world of difference between these two mind-sets.) Tom did not want to engage in an intelligent, fact-based conversation about ways to improve the company's recruiting efforts. Data simply did not appeal to him, especially when it conflicted with his existing beliefs and self-interest.

On a different level, I suspected that Tom didn't appreciate what he perceived to be my precociousness. He had far more experience in recruiting and had worked at Beneke for a decade longer than I had. No matter how tactfully I tried to present my findings, who was I—a recent hire just out of grad school—to tell him that he was going about his job in precisely the wrong way? In fairness to me, and to quote Bill Ackman, "Who says you have to be old to be good?"

Tom faced no penalty for ignoring analytics. On the contrary, he had plenty of company at Beneke and in HR. As I saw during my tenure there, Beneke tolerated this indifference and *even open hostility* to data and analytics. In other words, Tom and his ilk weren't iconoclasts. I was. Disillusioned with the culture, I left the company within a year.

---

* Mind you, I have no axe to grind with Big Red. I attended Cornell from 1995 to 1997 and received my master's in industrial and labor relations. I joke with my colleagues that no one has a less relevant degree to teach in the Department of Information Systems.

RESULTS AND LESSONS

As far as I know, Tom continued to visit Ivy League schools and employ the same analytics-free approach to recruiting. My findings didn't change his mind-set one iota. I stayed in touch with a few friends at Beneke after I left and we chewed the fat every so often. Ultimately, individuals who believed in the power of data and analytics didn't last much longer than I did.

As for lessons, the Beneke case study is instructive on a number of levels. It proves that many people, departments, and even entire companies still don't get it. If you're reading this book, then it's reasonable to conclude that you value analytics or are at least open to analytics as a concept. Don't assume that everyone does—let alone equally. Plenty of people talk the talk without walking the walk.

Remember Chapter 8: The contrast between the two HR leaders there and Beneke's HR leader in this chapter could not have been starker. At Google, Laszlo Bock and his team went where the data took them. If that meant changing longstanding company beliefs and policies such as using GPA as a hiring criterion, then so be it.

On an organizational level, Google demonstrated how analytics can result in disproving faulty assumptions that, in turn, improve business outcomes. Lamentably, Beneke showed the opposite: firms often ignore inconvenient yet compelling data to their detriment.

CHAPTER REVIEW AND DISCUSSION QUESTIONS

- Describe the general approach to analytics in HR at Beneke Pharmaceuticals. Did its employees embrace analytics?
- When it comes to making recruiting decisions, how does Beneke differ from Google?
- Which company's approach is better? Why?
- How do analytics threaten established professionals?
- What are you going to do when—not if—someone doesn't want to listen to the data and analytics that you've prepared?

NEXT

The next case study shows how an Agile mind-set can help tackle even the thorniest data conundrums. We also discover how two entities tried to solve the same business problem in two very different ways: Agile versus Waterfall.

Guess which one emerges victorious.

CHAPTER 10

Ice Station Zebra Medical

How Agile Methods Solved a Messy Health-Care Data Problem

The journey of a thousand miles begins with one step.

—Lao Tzu

I n the summer of 2008, a group of employees filed a lawsuit against a multisite health-care system. (I call that organization *Ice Station Zebra Medical* or *ISZM* here, although it's a pseudonym.*)

---

* As well as an obscure *Breaking Bad* and *Better Call Saul* reference.

The crux of the matter: ISZM had systematically underpaid over-time to thousands of its current and former nurses over the past decade. The employees' attorneys alleged that ISZM owed their plain-tiffs potentially millions of dollars in back pay, interest, and penalties. In the process, ISZM may have violated the Fair Labor Standards Act. Beyond that, the lawyers intimated that the U.S. Department of Labor might be interested in what was going on there.

PAYING NURSES

Odds are that you don't know a great deal about paying nurses. I doubt that you've ever thought about it. Sure, you imagine, they can take sick, vacation, and holiday pay like the rest of us. That's true, but things quickly diverge. No, the process is not "rocket surgery" and it hardly rivals Google's almighty search algorithm. Still, paying nurses is far more complicated than paying the average layperson.

With rare exception, hospitals do not compensate their nurses based on fixed, 40-hour "regular" workweeks, occasionally tap-ping into their paid time off plans. On the contrary, many other factors are at play with these folks. (For this very reason, most large health-care organizations have purchased and deployed proper time-keeping and scheduling software such as Kronos or Ceridian. These applications rely on complex matrices that account for many scenarios, and ultimately get these numbers right.) For now, suffice it to say that nurses typically receive different rates of pay and/or premiums based on:

- Time worked (shift differentials)
- Length of shift (8 versus 12 hours)
- Whether they needed to be available while not at work (on-call pay)
- Whether they "floated" (traveled to different hospitals)
- The specific days on which they worked—that is, holiday, weekend, etc.

Table 10.1 shows fictitious payroll data for a nurse on a single day.

Table 10.1 Generic Nurse Payroll Data

Employee_ID	Date	Pay_Code	Time_In	Time_Out	Hours	Rate
1234	1/1/08	REG	04:00	08:30	4.00	$20.00
1234	1/1/08	REG	09:30	13:30	6:00	$20.00
1234	1/1/08	SHIFT1	04:00	08:30	4.50	$2.00
1234	1/1/08	ON-CALL	12:00	04:00	4.00	$5.00
1234	1/1/08	OVT	11:30	13:30	2.00	$30.00

Source: Phil Simon.

Note that the five records in Table 10.1 reflect only a single nurse's pay on a single day—and a simplified version at that.* Multiply this number by 250 workdays per year by thousands of nurses for, say, 10 years. It should be no surprise that payroll tables in large hospital systems can easily reach tens of millions of records.

Even against this backdrop, you might think that responding to the overtime lawsuit would be a simple matter. Couldn't an ISZM payroll manager or finance director just click a mouse a few times? Couldn't a system's standard report easily determine how much employee overtime the organization paid its employees? More generally, didn't ISZM possess the data to nip this lawsuit in the bud?

Again, you would think so—and you would be spectacularly wrong. Because of myriad system, data, personnel, and organizational issues, ISZM was hamstrung. It could not answer basic data-oriented questions such as:

- Which employees received overtime pay, when, and how much?
- Did ISZM pay overtime to its employees correctly?
- Did different hospitals in the system pay overtime consistently?
- Finally, what was the difference—if any—between the overtime that employees actually received and should have received? And could the hospital prove that to a bunch of attorneys chomping at the bit to go to court?

---

*I have seen as many as 30 different records for a single nurse's daily pay.

ENTER THE CONSULTANT

This is where I came in. At that time in my career, I had worked extensively with a number of leading HR, payroll, and timekeeping applications, including several that ISZM used. I had done plenty of "front end" work in the form of system configuration and testing, troubleshooting, and end-user system training. Unlike most functional consultants, however, I was skilled at extracting data from—and manipulating data in—contemporary relational databases (aka the "back end"). I knew how to write complex reports and identify data-related issues.

Even better, I had worked with ISZM's finance director Terri (another pseudonym) on a previous engagement. We got along well and she held me in high regard. Terri contacted me for help and asked if I was available to assist her in answering these pressing questions—and fast.

It turns out that I could, but it would not be easy.

Over the course of four months, I talked to ISZM's different payroll personnel. I read arcane pay sections of union contracts that specified in excruciating detail what counted as overtime and what did not. I began to understand ISZM systems by consuming policy documents and different data dictionaries.* I try to locate entity-relationship diagrams† of ISZM's legacy systems. Sadly, in many cases, they didn't exist.

You might be wondering why I had to go hunting. Most of ISZM's hospitals had used different systems and pay codes in the past. Because of this, I couldn't just pull consistent data out of a single database. I knew that I would need to create my own translation or "XLAT" tables to compare apples to oranges. I built week-specific tables because different hospitals abided by different pay and work periods. That is, Hospital A's pay period might end every Friday while Hospital B's pay period always ends on Tuesday. Finally, to maximize speed, I created several database views.‡

---

* A data dictionary explains the general structure of a database, relationships among tables, and the definitions of each field. As such, it is invaluable on these types of projects.
† These are visual representations showing how database tables are connected or, in database parlance, *joined*.
‡ Database views are typically smaller versions of proper tables. That is, they contain fewer fields and records. As such, queries from them run faster.

I won't bore you with any more technical details, but my project at ISZM was no picnic and the stakes were high. For instance, a simple date error, transposed value, or mislabeled or missing pay code could mean tens or hundreds of thousands of dollars paid out incorrectly—*or not paid out at all*. If Terri couldn't get a handle on the situation, she may have found herself out of a job.

But where to begin?

USER STORIES

After meeting with ISZM personnel and understanding their needs, I developed the following user stories:

- As the head of finance, I need to be able to run summary reports to determine how much money each department owes.
- As the head of finance, I need to be able to run department detail reports to answer executives' questions about specific employees.
- As the head of finance, I need to be able to run individual summary reports to determine how much money we owe each employee.
- As a payroll manager, I need to be able to run individual detail reports to answer employee questions.
- As a payroll clerk, I need to view employee payroll information by data range to answer employee questions.

For a project of this complexity, I never considered using the Waterfall method. Boiling the ocean was not an option here, and I wasn't a fan of the technique anyway. Even an experienced system consultant like myself could not sit in a room, work independently, and emerge two or three months later with the answer. A single missed assumption or misinterpreted business rule might render my entire model moot and send me back to the drawing board. Plus, I wanted Terri to know what I was doing and why—at least at a high level. If I was on the wrong track, she was uniquely qualified to tell me so.

In short, I needed to employ Agile methods.

Every week I met with Terri, updating her on my progress and pending issues. Beyond that, I would find time on her schedule if I reached critical points that necessitated her input. Yes, looking at reams of nurse payroll data provided me with valuable insights into ISZM's pay practices, but I lacked critical institutional knowledge that only Terri and her staff could provide.

By the end of the first month, I had developed an admittedly rudimentary application, shown in Figure 10.1.

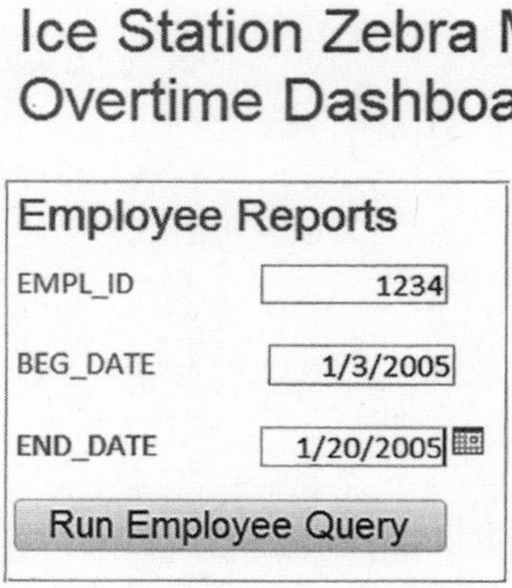

Figure 10.1 Front End for ISZM Microsoft Access Application, Version 1.0
Source: Phil Simon.

In keeping with Agile methods, the first iteration was simple by design. I knew that I had more user stories to tackle, but they would come later. I gave Terri several detailed reports on sample nurses to see if my assumptions were sound. It turns out that they were.

Of course, Terri needed to run payroll reports on *groups* of employees. She wanted department-level reporting by date range. Confident that I was on right track after version 1.0, I added that functionality to the next iteration. Figure 10.2 shows version 1.1 of the Access application.

As she nodded in approval at the numbers, I felt emboldened to add to the back end new hospitals, departments, data sources, employees, pay codes, and the like. On the front end (i.e., the reporting dashboard), I kept adding reports and data that Terri and the other ISZM users requested. For instance, Terri needed to verify which nurses and

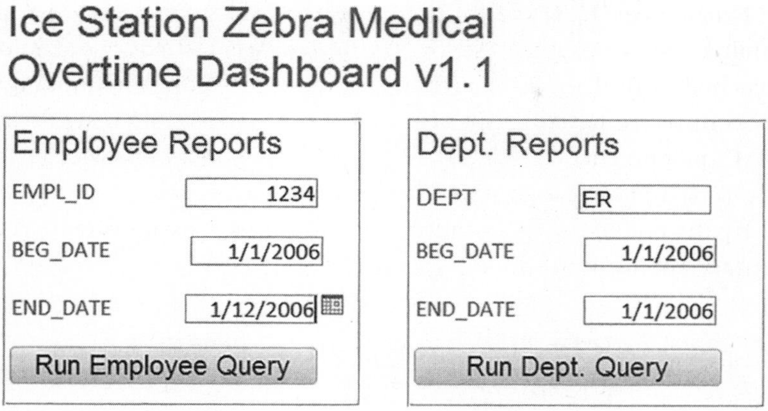

Ice Station Zebra Medical Overtime Dashboard v1.1

Employee Reports		Dept. Reports	
EMPL_ID	1234	DEPT	ER
BEG_DATE	1/1/2006	BEG_DATE	1/1/2006
END_DATE	1/12/2006	END_DATE	1/1/2006
Run Employee Query		Run Dept. Query	

Figure 10.2 Front End for ISZM Microsoft Access Application, Version 1.1
Source: Phil Simon.

departments did *not* receive overtime in a given time period. I built those reports and added them to version 1.2 of the app, shown in Figure 10.3.

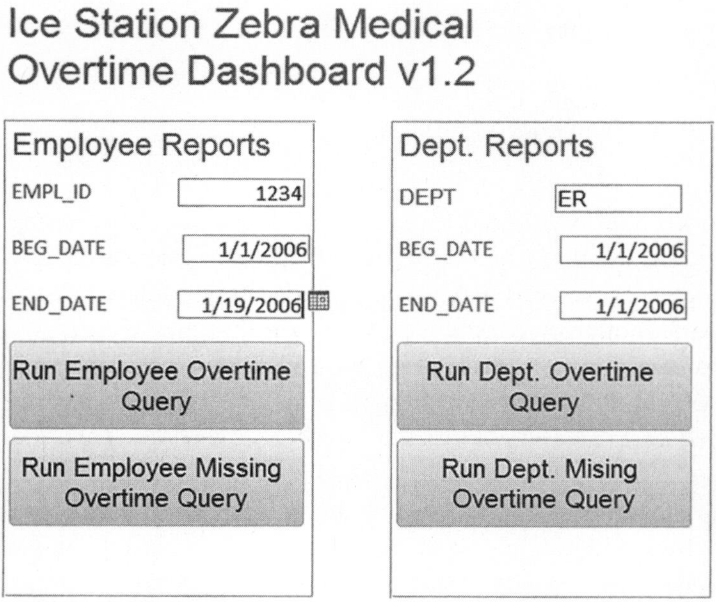

Ice Station Zebra Medical Overtime Dashboard v1.2

Employee Reports		Dept. Reports	
EMPL_ID	1234	DEPT	ER
BEG_DATE	1/1/2006	BEG_DATE	1/1/2006
END_DATE	1/19/2006	END_DATE	1/1/2006
Run Employee Overtime Query		Run Dept. Overtime Query	
Run Employee Missing Overtime Query		Run Dept. Mising Overtime Query	

Figure 10.3 Front End for ISZM Microsoft Access Application, Version 1.2
Source: Phil Simon.

Terri's stress level started to diminish. She even laughed at a few of my jokes. By involving her throughout the development and analysis process, I was cementing her initial trust. The same cannot be said about another group.

AGILE: THE BETTER WAY

To keep the story simple, I intentionally omitted one key detail of my work at ISZM until now: I wasn't working alone—not exactly, anyway. When I started, ISZM had concurrently hired a prestigious and pricey consultancy to try to solve the same employee-overtime riddle. (I call that firm *Badger* here, but it's another pseudonym.)

Terri's rationale made complete sense:

- For such a complicated problem, why not separate church and state?
- Why not put two knowledgeable and *independent* entities on the same project?
- Hiring a technology and audit firm showed the plaintiffs' attorneys that ISZM was taking the issue seriously.

Badger dutifully sent a team of three full-time consultants to ISZM. A partner also dropped in from time to time. Unlike me, the Badger folks followed the traditional Waterfall method and attempted to boil the ocean.

As the project progressed, I began to sense that Badger's hired guns were struggling mightily. These consultants were friendly but clearly out of their element. Frequent pop-ins to my office clued me in. When I politely reminded them that we were supposed to be working independently, they demurred. Badger's project manager even tried to charm me with obvious compliments and promises of future consulting opportunities.

Terri couldn't believe that a single person (me) was making so much progress while a team of three supposed experts was floundering. Badger's weekly bill was more than five times higher than mine. By the end of the second month, Terri's patience was wearing thin.

Ultimately, Badger failed miserably. Its consultants never had a chance to succeed: The consultancy didn't send the right folks for the job and, to boot, didn't follow Agile methods. Mismatched personnel who follow a dated game plan rarely get the job done.

RESULTS

Alright, I'll cut to the chase. It took me nearly four months, but I solved ISZM's thorny data problem. I created a user-friendly tool that allowed nontechnical users to query remarkably complex data, receive answers to their questions, and export the results to any format they liked. In Scrum terms, I completed each user story. Terri was pleased with my work, and although I no longer do that type of consulting, I can count on her as a reference.

Ultimately, my Microsoft Access application pulled together dozens of data sources and easily used 100 different tables—many of which I needed to build myself given the nature of the project. The final routine took more than three hours to run for the entire hospital system, but anyone could run it. Knowing that Terri and her employees were no database mavens, I made sure that she could easily run reports by employee, department, hospital, and date range with a few keystrokes.

LESSONS

Remember two things from this chapter. First, Agile methods can work on all sorts of data-related projects. That is, they don't need to fall under the umbrella of proper *analytics*. Second, small can beat big. A single person with superior system knowledge employing more contemporary methods can accomplish more than an entire team whose members cling to old ways. That is, by embracing the power of small batches and rapid iterations, David can defeat Goliath.

CHAPTER REVIEW AND DISCUSSION QUESTIONS

- Why was perfoming business discovery so critical at ISZM?
- What was the state of the data at ISZM? How did it get this way?
- Why was collecting its data so problematic? What was the biggest issue?
- What were the benefits of involving Terri and her team throughout the process?
- Did the presence of a separate team help or hinder ISZM? Why or why not?
- Why did the Badger consultants fail? What should they have done differently?

NEXT

To be sure, analyzing messy historical data under the pressure of a possible class-action lawsuit is stressful. Sure, the matter was still private, but the meter is always running and a single mistake can cost millions of dollars. However, solving a largely *retrospective* data or analytics puzzle in private isn't the same as dealing with a real-time, racially charged crisis unfolding in the media.

The next chapter shows how one company skillfully handled itself in the midst of such a maelstrom.

CHAPTER 11

Racial Profiling at Nextdoor

Using Data to Build a Better App and Combat a PR Disaster

Action expresses priorities.

—Mahatma Gandhi

By all accounts, Nirav Tolia seems like a generally jovial guy—and for good reason.

Tolia cofounded the "hyperlocal" social network Nextdoor in 2010 along with David Wiesen, Prakash Janakiraman, and Microsoft veteran Sarah Leary. Today, he serves as its CEO.

If you haven't heard of it, Nextdoor is a useful app that fills a genuine need that Facebook does not: to connect with our neighbors. Today, millions of people in over 140,000 "microcommunities" use it.* Tolia has been front and center spreading the company gospel. Media appearances have flowed, including an appearance on *Dr. Phil.*†

Tolia had to be downright giddy on March 3, 2015, when his company announced that it had raised $110 million in venture capital. The deal valued the company at more than $1 billion. Champagne all around: Nextdoor had reached the revered status of *unicorn.*

A scant three weeks later, all of that celebrating must have seemed like a distant memory. The news site Fusion published an article explaining how Nextdoor "is becoming a home for racial profiling."[1] As Pendarvis Harshaw wrote:

> While Nextdoor's ability to assist in crime-spotting has been celebrated as its "killer feature" by tech pundits, the app is also facilitating some of the same racial profiling we see playing out in cities across the country. Rather than bridging gaps between neighbors, Nextdoor can become a forum for paranoid racialism—the equivalent of the nosy Neighborhood Watch appointee in a gated community.[2]

Harshaw detailed how presumably white members were using Nextdoor's crime and safety forum to report "suspicious" activities by African Americans and Latinos. Harshaw's article included redacted screen shots from ignorant or hateful Nextdoor users such as the one in Figure 11.1.

casing the house

████████████████████████████████

we just had a young AA woman with long dreds very slender and light (should have been in school) knock aggressively on our door and ask for "keith". first time while we were home.she disappeared immediately after. checked all cross streets.

████████████████████████████████

Figure 11.1 Screenshot from Racially Charged User
Source: Fusion.‡

---

* See https://nextdoor.com/find-neighborhood.
† Watch it at http://bit.ly/2nvo6Gh.
‡ See http://fus.in/1N4GrOF.

Not long after Harshaw's article went live, Tolia and his senior team soon entered disaster and damage-control mode. This was the type of story that had legs. Case in point: Less than two months later, Jennifer Medina of the *New York Times* continued the thread, reporting that:

> . . . as Nextdoor has grown, users have complained that it has become a magnet for racial profiling, leading African-American and Latino residents to be seen as suspects in their own neighborhoods.[3]

How Nextdoor responded illustrates the importance of reacting quickly and how Agile analytics can be invaluable in this regard.

UNINTENDED BUT FAMILIAR CONSEQUENCES

Why didn't Tolia and his team see this type of abuse coming?

Such a question might seem obvious, but it is inherently unfair.

As the cliché goes, hindsight is 20/20. No one could have reasonably expected Nextdoor to launch its app with every conceivable feature and safeguard already in place. That's not very pragmatic and it certainly isn't very Agile.

In a way, Nextdoor had become a victim of its own success. Racial profiling wouldn't have become a problem on the app if few people had downloaded and used it. (Yes, there are drawbacks to network effects.) After all, most start-ups fail; few ever attain anywhere near Nextdoor's level of reach.

As BackChannel's Jessi Hempel wrote:

> Most social web services—like Airbnb or Facebook or Twitter—were launched quickly. Their founding teams— consisting mostly of well-off men (and the occasional woman) from prestigious universities—were not diverse. Those teams hired designers and engineers who looked like them to launch and grow the sites. These companies weren't thinking about the way bias would influence how people use their services; they were moving fast and breaking things, content to fill in the details later. What's more, they mostly built advertising businesses that became

more successful as people provided them more social data by posting more on the sites. There was little business incentive for them to slow their users down and ask them to think about why and how they were posting—and, in some cases, to post less.[4]

Like just about all startups these days, Nextdoor initially focused on growth. As Figure 11.2 shows, the app included basic reporting functionality, but it wasn't particularly sophisticated.

Figure 11.2 Screenshot from Original Nextdoor App
Source: Nextdoor.

Nevertheless, Nextdoor was starting to grow up. It now was a unicorn, not the pipedream of a few ambitious college students who are, as another hackneyed Silicon Valley phrase goes, looking to "make the world a better place." Big-boy companies face big-boy problems.

EVALUATING THE PROBLEM

Nextdoor could have easily taken a *laissez-faire* stance to charges of allowing racial profiling on its app. Its founders could have rationalized that no site or app is perfect, that fleas come with the dog, and so on.

There's plenty of historical precedent for maintaining such a position. The tech landscape is littered with founders who claim that their products are merely neutral conduits that facilitate communication or commerce among users. Consider some examples over the years:

- Google and Yahoo long turned a blind eye to click fraud. Google also took its sweet time addressing copyright-infringement claims on YouTube.
- eBay launched without any formal buyer protection, and even today, many users find it wanting.
- Facebook's leadership allowed fake news to proliferate on the social media site during the 2016 U.S. presidential election.
- Unlike hotels, Airbnb assumes no responsibility for the safety of its guests. To this end, the company has quietly settled lawsuits that would have resulted in devastating press.*
- Uber has steadfastly refused to conduct background checks on drivers, something that taxi companies have done for decades.
- Twitter, for years, let trolls and terrorist groups operate unabated. (For more on this, see "ESP at Twitter" in Chapter 2.)

To its credit, Nextdoor's actions distinguished the company from its largely apathetic tech brethren. Its management immediately addressed the problem of racial bias head-on. Perhaps Tolia and Jana-kiraman (Indian Americans) and Leary (a woman) were particularly sensitive to the issue because they didn't look like most start-up founders. It's conceivable—maybe even probable—that they would not have moved as quickly had they been white males, à la Travis Kalanick of Uber. The cofounders might have feared that negative press would harm their individual reputations, not to mention Nextdoor's eye-popping valuation. Maybe it was a combination of all of these things.

Whatever its motivations, Nextdoor moved quickly. The cofounders assembled a small but diverse team to tackle the issue. Members included product head Maryam Mohit, communications director Kelsey Grady, a product manager, a designer, a data scientist, and later, a software engineer. (Chapter 5 showed how Agile teams benefit from different perspectives, skills, and expertise.)

Within five months, the team believed that it had found an answer to its problem. Its three-pronged solution included diversity training

* See Brad Stone's book *The Upstarts*.

for its neighborhood operations team as well as an update to its community guidelines and an accompanying blog post. The third part,
though, proved to be the trickiest.

Redesigning the App

Nextdoor understood the intimate nexus among app design and user
behavior and data. The design of any app directly affects how users
interact with it as well as the data it generates. Change the app's design
and you probably change user behavior—as well as the types of data
that users generate.

By way of background, Nextdoor for years had allowed people to
flag inappropriate posts, either by content or location. For instance,
commercial posts don't belong in noncommercial areas of the app/
website. Nextdoor realized that a binary (i.e., flagged or not flagged)
was no longer sufficient. To this end, the company added a quick fix in
the form of a *report racial profiling* button.

Ultimately, this step was woefully inadequate because many users
didn't understand the new feature. Identifying racial profiling isn't
tantamount to spotting a red Lexus sedan speeding down the street.
"Nextdoor members began reporting all kinds of unrelated slights as
racial profiling. 'Somebody reported her neighbor for writing mean
things about pit bulls,' Mohit recall[ed]."[5]

Much of Nextdoor's data was text-centric (i.e., unstructured).
Especially at first, this type of data doesn't lend itself to the kind of
easy analysis that its more structured equivalent makes possible. This
difficulty doubles when trying to deal with a thorny issue like race
relations. Tolia and his colleagues understood this and assigned five
employees to read through thousands of user posts. The course of
action was anything but obvious.

By looking at the data, the team grasped that it needed to take a
step back and answer a core question: What exactly *is* racial profiling
anyway? As Hempel wrote:

> The team realized it needed to help users understand when
> to use race when talking about suspicious or criminal
> activity. And to do that, they needed to define—very
> specifically—what constituted racial profiling in the first
> place. "We could not find a definition of racial profiling that

everyone agreed on," says Tolia. "If you go to the NAACP, if you go to the ACLU, if you go to the White House Task Force on Diversity, if you go to the Neighbors for Racial Justice, none of these people agree on what racial profiling is."

An overly broad definition of racial profiling would capture far too many false positives. Conversely, an overly granular one would result in legitimate claims slipping through the cracks. Drawing the line would be neither simple nor easy. This recognition led Nextdoor management to ask fundamental questions about what it was trying to achieve and how:

- What if Nextdoor redesigned its reporting feature to gently guide its users in a specific direction?
- Could it design the app in a way to minimize and discourage the very behavior that it was attempting to prevent?
- Would better design ultimately lead to better data?
- Did one size really fit all? Was it time to separate *suspicious activity* from *crime and safety*?

Agile Methods in Action

We've seen throughout this book that Agile methods explicitly acknowledge uncertainty: It's usually impossible to know the path to success *in advance*. As Silicon Valley serial-entrepreneur and academician Steve Blank is fond of saying, "There are no facts inside your building." The implication is that no one can know what will work in a vacuum. Get outside the building, start testing, gather data, talk to users, and then you can evaluate your progress.

Nextdoor's top brass clearly understands this key tenet. To this end, the team developed six different variants of its app and began testing them. Doing so helped the company home in on the answers to key questions:

- If the app alerted users about the potential for racial bias before they posted, would it change user behavior?
- Characterizing a person isn't necessarily easy. How does an application prompt its users for descriptions of others that are full, fair, and, crucially, not based exclusively on race?
- In describing a suspicious person, how many attributes are enough? Which specific attributes are more important than others?

In keeping with methods espoused in *The Lean Startup*, the team conducted a series of A/B tests. Blessed with a sufficiently large user base, Nextdoor ran experiments to determine the right answers to these questions. For instance, consider two groups of 25,000 users divided into cohorts (A and B). Each group would see one version of the Nextdoor app with slight but important differences in question wording, order, required fields, and the like. As anyone with a modicum of knowledge in survey design knows, even the order of words can sway results.

Over the course of three months, Nextdoor's different permutations started to bear fruit. The team began to clarify the best way to address racial profiling. Certain versions of the app worked far better than others in this regard. Nextdoor was getting close. By August 2015, the team was ready to launch a new posting protocol in its crime and safety section—one far more granular than that shown in Figure 11.2.

As Figure 11.3 shows, users who mention race when posting to "Crime & Safety" forums now must provide additional information. Nextdoor requires users to enter a minimum of two of the following four additional categories: hair, top clothing, bottom clothing, and shoes. Figure 11.4 shows this redesigned form.

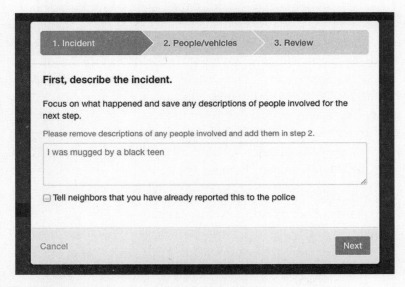

Figure 11.3 Screenshot from Nextdoor's Redesigned App
Source: Nextdoor.

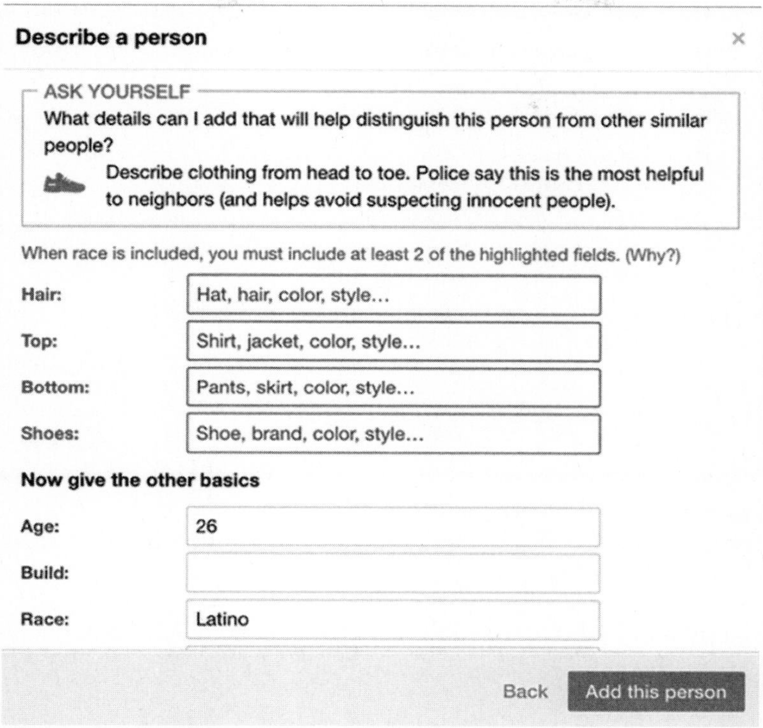

Describe a person   ✕

┌─ ASK YOURSELF ──
What details can I add that will help distinguish this person from other similar
people?
    Describe clothing from head to toe. Police say this is the most helpful
    to neighbors (and helps avoid suspecting innocent people).
└──

When race is included, you must include at least 2 of the highlighted fields. (Why?)

Hair: Hat, hair, color, style…

Top: Shirt, jacket, color, style…

Bottom: Pants, skirt, color, style…

Shoes: Shoe, brand, color, style…

Now give the other basics

Age: 26

Build:

Race: Latino

                                              Back   Add this person

Figure 11.4 Screenshot from Nextdoor's Redesigned App
Source: Nextdoor.

Before users can post suspicious activity, Nextdoor intentionally inserts additional friction.

None of this was coincidental; everything here was deliberate. No, Nextdoor will not eliminate posts by racist users with axes to grind or generally insensitive folks. It has, however, used data intelligently to redesign its product with fantastic results. Kudos to the company and its management for taking this issue so seriously and acting accordingly.

RESULTS AND LESSONS

Nextdoor was able to stem the bleeding in a relatively short period of time. (These matters are nuanced and quite difficult to fix.) By taking a data-oriented approach to design (illustrated in Figure 11.5), the

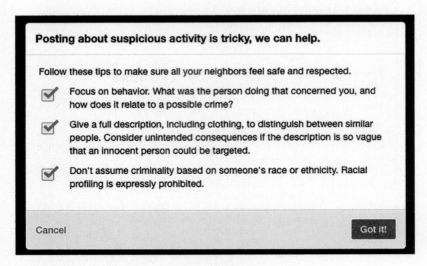

Figure 11.5 Screenshot from Nextdoor's Redesigned App
Source: Nextdoor.

company reported that it had reduced racial profiling by 75 percent. As Kashmir Hill wrote for *Fusion*:

> Erasing racism through technology alone is impossible, but Nextdoor found that a few changes to its interface actually did significantly discourage racial profiling by its users. All users who make posts to their neighborhood's "Crime and Safety" forum are now asked for additional information if their post mentions race. Nextdoor says that the new forms it's introducing have "reduced posts containing racial profiling by 75% in our test markets."[6]

If you think Nextdoor's new protocol adds friction that reduces the number of inappropriate user entries, you're absolutely right. Nextdoor reported that posts under suspicious activity dropped by 25 percent. As Tolia points out, though, "many of those posts shouldn't have been on the site in the first place."[7]

A lesser organization would have announced plans to "study the problem" as it continued unabated. Nextdoor unquestionably gained tremendous goodwill among many of its users by addressing what could have been an existential crisis. To be fair, it might have upset and even lost users who wanted to continue racial profiling, but the company is happy to make this trade-off.

CHAPTER REVIEW AND DISCUSSION QUESTIONS

- How did Nextdoor's first version of its app enable racial profiling?
- Was the fix simple? Why or why not?
- What do Nextdoor's changes mean in terms of the data that it now collects?
- Do you think that Nextdoor is finished tinkering with its app? Why or why not?
- What has the company learned from the experience? Will these lessons inform its future design decisions? Why or why not?

NEXT

We've covered a wide range of case studies. It is now time to switch gears and distill some of the lessons from Part Two.

NOTES

1. Pendarvis Harshaw, "Nextdoor, the Social Network for Neighbors, Is Becoming a Home for Racial Profiling," *Fusion*, March 24, 2015, http://fus.in/1N4GrOF.
2. Ibid.
3. Jennifer Medina, "Website Meant to Connect Neighbors Hears Complaints of Racial Profiling," *New York Times*, May 18, 2016, http://nyti.ms/2nREOAl.
4. Jessi Hempel, "For Nextdoor, Eliminating Racism Is No Quick Fix," *Backchannel*, February 16, 2017, http://bit.ly/2lR91PU.
5. Ibid.
6. Kashmir Hill, "How Nextdoor Reduced Racist Posts by 75%," *Fusion*, August 25, 2016, http://fus.in/2bA9XBG.
7. Hempel, "For Nextdoor, Eliminating Racism Is No Quick Fix."

PART **FOUR**

Making the Most Out of Agile Analytics

I n Part Four, we learn about the benefits, drawbacks, and limitations of Agile analytics. We also cover the importance of designing software applications specifically with data and analytics in mind.

This part includes the following chapters:

- **Chapter 12:** The Benefits of Agile Analytics: The Upsides of Small Batches
- **Chapter 13:** No Free Lunch: The Impediments to—and Limitations of—Agile Analytics
- **Chapter 14:** The Importance of Designing for Data: Lessons from the Upstarts

The Benefits of Agile Analytics

The Upsides of Small Batches

A little axe can cut down a big tree.

—Jamaican proverb

Across the board, Agile methods such as Scrum are generally superior to Waterfall-based methods. We know this, but now it's time to dive a bit deeper. This chapter describes how Scrum can specifically benefit organizations' analytic efforts. For the sake of simplicity, this chapter illustrates the benefits of Agile analytics by contrasting two large fictional organizations.

Let's begin with Ideal Agile Company (IAC). About 10 years ago, it shifted its software-development efforts by replacing the Waterfall method with Scrum. The results have been spectacular. IAC's data is pristine and comprehensive. Years ago, IAC deployed a master data management application. Recently, it embraced Agile analytics. IAC's culture is dynamic and very data- and analytics-oriented. One way or another, data drives most of IAC's business decisions.

LIFE AT IAC

Because of its success with Scrum with software development, the idea of applying similar Agile methods at IAC to a related area (i.e., analytics) wasn't weird; it was natural. (Ditto for the framework detailed in Chapter 6.) In fact, the company's prior success with Scrum in one discipline made it more likely to achieve success in another. As we see in this section, Scrum's benefits have been manifold, substantial, and most important, *sustained*.

Agile methods allow employees at IAC to quickly gain valuable insights and respond to crises. Time and time again, IAC sees these little victories. They allow its teams to acquire—and act on—valuable knowledge. Beyond that, its Agile projects aren't "chasing the money." If IAC needs to change course, it is more politically palatable for its executives. They can easily walk away from small sunk costs.

Data and Data Quality

At their core, all analytics projects—whether Agile or phase-gate—rely on data. At the risk of oversimplifying, better, more accurate, and more robust data leads to better analytics.

IAC has practiced Agile methods for years. Because employees regularly use data to make decisions, data is generally clean and ready to go. (Employees who shun data quality don't last long.) As such, IAC employees are ready to act quickly. They soon see the benefits that analytics yield.

In keeping with Agile methods, IAC's top brass recognizes that it is never going to get all desired data—not at first, not ever. Because future iterations (i.e., sprints and releases) are coming *soon*, employees do not place enormous pressure on themselves to "stick the landing." In turn, they know that their analytics will consistently improve in much the same way that their software has.

❓TIP

Generally speaking, the older and less used the data, the harder and more time-consuming it is to cleanse.

Insightful, Robust, and Dynamic Models

Equipped with excellent enterprise data, IAC employees plug into different APIs. In other words, they can start to look *outside* the enterprise for additional insights. Forget time saved to cleanse data. IAC is thus able to build more accurate, powerful, and generally better models than its competitors. Note that *better* doesn't mean *more complex*. As Chapter 6 notes (see "Model the Data"), a complicated model doesn't necessarily trump a simple one. All things being equal, however, better models will yield better results.

IAC employees develop models and determine from the get-go if they point in a general direction. A weak signal is often sufficient to proceed. Employees look for early proof that a data source, model, or specific variable is working, even if the weight or importance of that measure is still nebulous. Small, early hits provide enthusiasm to keep proceeding in a particular route. Because of its confidence in finding new and improved analytics and data sources, IAC isn't afraid to retire those that no longer serve a useful purpose.

❓TIP

Don't be afraid to refine or retire previously helpful analytics.

A Smarter, Realistic, and Skeptical Workforce

IAC employees know full well that Agile projects are *supposed* to ship early. That is, they need not be "complete." Almost every project has yielded an immediate return—although those returns have often been small at first.

Scrum teams at IAC use simple Kanban boards. Employees enjoy moving user stories from the "in process" column to the "done" column. The process just feels good. In other words, people like to get things done. Updating a status column on a spreadsheet just doesn't provide the same sense of satisfaction.

IAC doesn't just listen to employee feedback; the company routinely acts upon it. Remember from Chapter 5, although *sprint backlogs* are fixed, *product backlogs* are not. The latter grow over the life of projects and may never end. When employees and teams see their users' stories, ideas, and work take effect, they feel a sense of pride and even excitement, and why shouldn't they? They see actual progress (see Figure 4.1) and think: What *else* can we do? This typically makes for better software and analytics.

We see this in the Introduction (see "The Need for Speedier Analytics"). Today more than ever, speed kills. The longer that it takes an organization to produce something of value (software, analytics, etc.), the less likely it is to reap its rewards.

IAC employees are generally quite invested in their projects and jobs. Because they feel a strong sense of ownership, they identify short- and long-term problems and ask intelligent questions. IAC has found that its Scrum team members have a propensity to question proven models, data sources, and methodologies.

Pete is a typical IAC employee. He recently participated in the launch of a new analytics tool. A vital member of a Scrum team, he usually makes meaningful contributions. He also suggests new user stories and potential data sources. IAC management knows that employees routinely involved in the development of an analytics tool—or analytics themselves, for that matter—aren't just marking time at work. They commit to their jobs in a far deeper manner.

❓TIP

The continual use of analytics can breed a healthy skepticism among employees. In an era of Big Data, a critical mind-set is tremendously valuable.

Summary

IAC has created a virtuous cycle for itself. Employees routinely use data and analytics to make decisions, but IAC employees are anything but complacent. They refine existing analytics and develop new ones. The bar for a replacement is high. If a measure doesn't lend itself to action and a specific decision, then why keep using it?

LIFE AT RDC

By way of contrast, Really Dysfunctional Company (RDC) faces a much tougher row to hoe than IDC. For years, RDC's market share has been dwindling. It has seen countless business opportunities vanish for good—gobbled up by a competitor. It has fumbled its last five major product launches and its stock has suffered for it.

Project Management

RDC's top brass incorrectly believes that Scrum is just for start-ups. Despite its declining performance, RDC nevertheless remains committed to the Waterfall method for both software development and analytics. As its hidebound CEO is fond of saying, "The devil you know is better than the devil you don't."

RDC has purchased expensive software licenses and attendant consulting and support agreements. Collectively, these have locked up considerable capital ranging from high six to seven figures on a dozen projects. The payoff from these projects comes at their culmination—if at all. Even after launching, major questions abound, including:

- How will RDC management know if its employees will actually use that expensive new application? (Or, as I've seen many times, will people simply revert to using a stalwart such as Microsoft Excel?)
- How will its employees know if they are collecting and using the right data?
- How do employees know if their models are generally sound?
- How will they be able to spot future trends and react to them?

The short answer to all of these queries is that they won't—even after RDC has spent a great deal of time, money, and effort.

Even worse, the company's projects often do not yield a positive return on investment. Those that do typically take 18 months or more. The company has abandoned about 30 percent of projects altogether and written off the expense. This dismal track record means that RDC's management doesn't possess the courage to junk projects and tools that cross the finish line—whether they are useful or not. Because of rampant data-quality issues, employees rarely know if a particular measure is useful anyway. (We return to these issues momentarily.)

 TIP

Organizations that need a year or more to deploy analytics tools may find that a once-promising window has closed.

Frustrated Employees

RDC's culture is downright stodgy. Average tenure is just shy of 25 years. Senior employees are by and large skeptical of the power of all of these newfangled data sources and analytics. Without exception, existing policy along with executive opinion and rank drive the company's critical business decisions.

In the past, newly hired RDC employees have suggested improvements. Admittedly, some of these were pretty obvious. Stuck in their ways, management routinely ignored the input of these younger employees. Disappointed, not long after most stopped offering these suggestions and left the company. As for those who remain, some spend months or years waiting for that "killer app" or killer analytics that will solve all of their problems. They are usually disappointed and become jaded.

Consider Donald, the quintessential RDC employee. Now an IT director, he has worked at the company for 21 years. He is technically a member of a few project steering committees. He checks in on a project's status every few months, but is generally "too busy" to be bothered beyond that. His effort—or lack thereof—typifies the mindset of RDC employees.

Data Quality, Internal Politics, and the Blame Game

Generally speaking, RDC's data is a mess. Case in point: Obtaining a complete and accurate master list of customers typically takes several weeks.

At least RDC management can take solace in the fact that it has plenty of company here. Most experienced enterprise-technology consultants have seen this movie dozens of times before. According to some estimates, employees involved in analytics projects spend a mind-boggling 80 percent of their time preparing data instead of gleaning insights.* Talk about needing to crawl before you can run. This is certainly the case with RDC: the company's data does not lend itself to immediately performing even basic analytics—never mind really worthwhile ones.

Because its data is so problematic, RDC is in no position to begin ambitious technology and analytics endeavors. Its CIO is reluctant to commit to expensive IT projects until heads from different lines of business begin to take ownership of their data. Execs in the latter group believe that IT should "own" the data. Put differently, the IT-Business Divide† is alive and well at RDC.

Most RDC employees justifiably lack confidence that they can develop new and improved analytics. As a result, IAC employees rely on antiquated analytics and data sources. No one wants to topple the house of cards. Even though the world has changed, the way that IAC looks at it has not. The company is stuck in a vicious cycle.

Summary

For RDC to make any real progress, it would have to climb a steep organizational learning curve. A phase-gate mind-set has permeated its culture for decades. Although Scrum is not complicated, it is dramatically different from the Waterfall method. Even if progressive new management takes over tomorrow, don't expect a new culture. After all, change takes time.

---

* For more on this, see https://www.youtube.com/watch?v=t9n9KeV-6NI.
† I have no shortage of thoughts on this matter: http://bit.ly/2nKXSAB.

COMPARING THE TWO

Now think about RDC and all of its data-related struggles. Which company—RDC or IAC—will be able to more quickly develop analytics and use them? Table 12.1 shows a simple comparison.

Table 12.1 Comparison between Two Companies

Area	Advantage	
	IAC	RDC
Existing familiarity with Scrum	✓	
Length of learning curve	✓	
Respond to crises	✓	
Identify to nascent trends	✓	
Data quality	✓	
Time needed for data-preparation effort	✓	
Time needed to identify and integrate new data sources	✓	
Realistic expectations re: analytics	✓	
Time needed to discern between real and vanity metrics	✓	
Invite ideas for improvement	✓	

Source: Phil Simon.

CHAPTER REVIEW AND DISCUSSION QUESTIONS

- Judging from IAC, what do you think are the most important benefits of Agile methods for analytics endeavors?
- How has IAC created a virtuous cycle?
- Now look at RDC. Why is it destined for failure?
- Which of the two companies is better equipped to capitalize on the opportunities that Agile analytics can yield? Why?

NEXT

IAC and RDC couldn't be more different. The contrast between the two reveals that Agile approaches to analytics offer significant benefits over their Waterfall-based counterparts.

No methodology, however, *guarantees* successful results. In fact, different types of people- and data-related issues can impede and even sabotage a progressive company's most promising analytics efforts— even Agile ones. This is the subject of Chapter 13.

No Free Lunch

The Impediments to—and Limitations of—Agile Analytics

Culture eats strategy for breakfast.

—Peter Drucker

Along with Part Three, Chapter 12 enumerates the benefits of adopting an Agile approach to analytics. Still, to claim that there are no downsides would be demonstrably false. As we see in this chapter, no deployment method guarantees a successful outcome.

Note that I place the issues in this chapter into two buckets: *people* and *data*. In reality, though, these distinctions aren't nearly so neat. For instance, data-quality issues plague many a firm because employees don't fully understand the importance of clean and comprehensive data.

PEOPLE ISSUES

Peter Drucker's quote at the beginning of this chapter holds a great deal of water. Despite great resources, many corporate initiatives spectacularly fail. In reality, some never had a chance of success because of cultural and people issues.

Resistance to Analytics

As powerful as data and analytics can be, they are often no match for human resistance. Remember that analytics generally don't do anything by themselves. Chapters 8 and 9 crystallize the profound cultural differences between Google and the apocryphal Beneke Pharmaceuticals. Fundamentally, Laszlo Bock embraced analytics while "Tom" actively *resisted* them.

Tom has plenty of company. Billy Beane of *Moneyball* fame routinely clashed with longtime scouts who were unwilling to even look at data. I know an acquisitions editor who refused to let his authors conduct A/B tests on book covers and titles because he empirically "knew" the best version of each. I have heard people emphatically state in meetings, "I don't need data to tell *me* what's going on!" If you haven't dealt with dataphobes such as these in your career, you soon will.

These people frustrate employees who appreciate the power of data and analytics. In fact, they are actually doing us a favor by tipping their hands because people resist data and analytics in many ways. Put differently, you need not *actively* declare war on the insights that data and analytics can provide. There are plenty of *passive* ways to effectively accomplish the same thing.

Generally speaking, you will find three types of people in the world:

1. Those who get it.
2. Those who don't get it but want to get it.
3. Those who don't get it and don't want to get it.

Ideally, everyone at your current or future employer falls into the first group, but that's very unlikely once an organization reaches a certain size. Vocal dataphobes such as the ones mentioned earlier are loudly and unequivocally placing themselves in that third group. Disagree all you like, but at least you know where they stand.

❓ TIP

Wouldn't you prefer to know the internal enemies of analytics? You could then focus your energy on the second group: the very ones who are willing to use data to attack problems in new ways.

Stakeholder Availability

Whether with software development or analytics, Agile methods only work when clients, key stakeholders, and subject-matter experts can routinely provide their time and input. Remember that Scrum is the antithesis of the Waterfall method. Stakeholders don't just attend a project kickoff meeting and see the final result one year later. On the contrary, they need to be involved early and often.

This does not mean that life stands still. People sometimes cancel meetings. Emergencies and other priorities often take precedence over planned work. In other words, life happens. Still, no Scrum team can be successful in a vacuum.

Unfortunately, I have seen plenty of clients and project sponsors go AWOL, especially on remote projects. The Scrum team is left trying to hit a moving target. As I argue throughout this book, Agile methods are superior to their phase-gate counterparts, but no method can overcome indifference to a project or its objectives.

Irritating Customers, Users, and Employees with Frequent Changes

Microsoft incurred the wrath of its customer base for Windows 8 by removing the iconic Start button. Not long before that, the company confused millions of users by revamping its user interface (UI) in Office 2007. The introduction of its new "ribbon" confounded many longtime Excel, Word, and PowerPoint users.

The same type of confusion can stem from companies that frequently change measures. Consider the following:

- What if Google revamped its algorithm every week? (I'm excluding minor changes.)
- What if Facebook overhauled its UI, privacy policy, and advertising measures every other day?
- What if your company constantly noodled with its annual bonus plan?

The point is that changes in data-related policies and analytics are going to take place: it's a matter of when, not if. Chapter 7 shows how the University Tutoring Center changed the way that it calculated tutor utilization several times. To state the obvious, companies need to really think these types of data-related changes through and, just as important, communicate them well.

DATA ISSUES

Some people understand the import of analytics. As such, their curious nature, availability to answer questions, and critical eye make them invaluable and a pleasure to work with. Success with analytics, however, doesn't just require the earnest intentions of those around you: your colleagues, superiors, clients, and underlings. Thorny data issues can stifle the efforts of "good people" (those in my first two groups).

 TIP

Good people are necessary but insufficient for success with analytics.

Data Quality

Some software applications offer a great sizzle factor. I've been in some tech product demos and clients' eyes have damn near popped out. I could almost see the light bulbs appear above their heads. They were barely able to contain their excitement. Oh, the possibilities!

Let's take a step back. One issue will invariably preclude those tchotchkes from delivering anywhere near their lofty potential. I'm talking here about data quality

I'll be the first to admit that it isn't the sexiest of topics, but it's a formidable beast. For as long as I can remember, professionals have used the acronym GIGO. It stands for "garbage in, garbage out." Corrupted data sources, blasé employees, and poorly designed business processes have thwarted many organizations' efforts to understand what is going on and then do something about it.

In the past, employees in different lines of business (LOBs) often pinned their organization's data-quality issues on the IT department. After all, the rationale went, these folks are singlehandedly responsible for the systems that store enterprise information.

Talk about blaming the messenger. It's ludicrous to blame IT when:

- Employees in different LOBs such as payroll and accounting routinely make data-entry errors.
- Senior executives design opaque organizational processes that their own employees don't fully understand.
- Department heads build and use their own applications without the knowledge of the IT department, let alone its consent. (This is often called shadow IT.)

Just about every large organization suffers from at least some of these problems. However, widespread data-quality issues cause many headaches. Generally speaking, they erode employees' trust in enterprise information; introduce doubt about the integrity of their systems; slow down, if not halt, the decision-making process; and, finally, introduce superfluous risk. What happens if we act on incorrect information?

❓TIP

Depending on the state of your organization's data quality, it may make sense to delay your analytics efforts.

Overfitting and Spurious Correlations

Countries with higher per-capital chocolate consumption are more likely to produce Nobel laureates.* You would be smart to feed your children loads of candy if you want them to be successful.

Over the past five years, the U.S. murder rate has dropped in near lockstep with the decline in the usage of Microsoft's Internet Explorer.† Looks like Google Chrome, Safari, and Firefox are saving lives!

Each of these assertions is patently ridiculous. The fact that these two sets of trends coincide with each other proves exactly nothing. The well-worn axiom is as valid as ever: Correlation does not equal causation. The immortal words of economist Ronald Coase express a similar sentiment: "If you torture the data enough, nature will always confess."‡ You are bound to find relationships among unrelated variables if you look hard enough, but that doesn't validate the relationships among them.

If you add hundreds of variables to a model, then you'll concurrently explain everything and nothing. In statistics, this notion is known as *overfitting*. It occurs when a model is excessively complex. Typically, this means that you're using too many variables and/or a tiny sample size.

Certain Problems May Call for a More Traditional Approach to Analytics

Although Agile methods generally deliver superior results to their Waterfall counterparts, there are instances in which the latter still make sense. Think about the software-development world for a moment. Initially launching a dating app such as Tinder with only a

---

* See www.nejm.org/doi/full/10.1056/NEJMon1211064.
† See http://read.bi/1i04dhq.
‡ People often cite this as "If you torture the data long enough, it will confess."

handful of features is prudent. Why spend a ton of time and money on a new app if you're not certain if people are going to download it—never mind actually use it? Only after gaining momentum is it wise to add bells and whistles. Tinder has done just that. Dropbox did the same thing with its file-sharing service, although its first release contained a great deal of functionality.* As Voltaire said, "The best is the enemy of the good."

But what about pharmaceuticals or automobiles? Products such as these don't lend themselves to a "launch now, fix later" approach. Even though Dropbox and Tinder launched with known limitations and even a few bugs, they weren't going to kill their users. Cars and drugs, though, are different animals. And the same holds true for analytics.

In some cases, it's imperative that analytics or a model be as accurate and comprehensive as possible. For instance, the fictional Gray Matter Systems (GMS) has lost a few of its highest-performing software engineers. GMS's management is justifiably concerned about further employee attrition. To stem the tide, it is toying with the idea of granting $30,000 retention bonuses and additional stock options to its most valuable and poachable employees. Should the company adopt an Agile approach?

Think about the significant downsides of this program. It's not hard to imagine several ways that this strategy could backfire. GMS could be:

- Handing oodles of cash to employees who have already mentally checked out.
- Granting unnecessary bonuses to employees who weren't thinking of leaving in the first place.
- Causing a rift among developers. "Why did Steven receive a bonus when I didn't? I'm just as good as he is."
- Alienating nondevelopers.

If GMS is unsure about whether its analytics support making such a business decision, then it's probably best to wait until it is much more confident in its numbers. Sometimes you only get one bite at the apple, or, put in another way, certain bells cannot be unrung.

---

* Watch it at https://www.youtube.com/watch?v=7QmCUDHpNzE.

THE LIMITATIONS OF AGILE ANALYTICS

Consider two organizations:

1. **ABC:** Develops analytics using the Waterfall method.
2. **XYZ:** Develops analytics using Agile methods.

Analytics: The Agile Way argues that, all else being equal, XYZ will be far more successful than ABC. That's a far cry, though, from saying that the use of Agile analytics *guarantees* success. It doesn't. The next section explains some of those limitations.

Acting Prematurely

In 2011, Israeli-American psychologist Daniel Kahneman released one of the most important psychology books in recent memory. *Thinking, Fast and Slow* draws heavily on his work with the cognitive and mathematical psychologist Amos Tversky. Kahneman (whom I met briefly in 2011 at a speaking engagement in Washington, D.C.) posited that our brains were divided into two systems:

- **System 1:** Produces the fast, intuitive reactions and instantaneous decisions that govern most of our lives. Let's say that you are attending a baseball game and your seat is near first base. A batter hits a foul ball at your head. The ball is traveling at more than 90 miles and your fight-or-flight instinct takes over. You get out of the way. Congratulations, you just invoked System 1!
- **System 2:** Produces more deliberate and reasoned thinking— a.k.a., *analysis*. If you play Sudoku, Scrabble, or crossword puzzles, you are invoking System 2.

Kahneman noted that we need *both* systems to survive because each serves a key purpose.

Analytics is an amalgam of both systems as well. The process of *developing* analytics generally requires System 2 thinking because there's so much data today. *Acting* on analytics, though, often lends itself to System 1 thinking.

Still, there's a real danger in mechanically taking action just because the data tells you to do so. On May 6, 2010, U.S. stock indexes collectively lost more than $1 trillion. Dubbed the *Flash Crash*, sophisticated algorithms of high-frequency trading firms swapped thousands of stocks each instant—just as *they were programmed to do*. To make a long story short: one bad trade nearly set off another financial meltdown.*

Stories such as these underscore one of the cardinal truths of data and analytics: Never mistake *can* with *should*. Even when confronted with seemingly incontrovertible data and analytics, it is imperative to remember System 2. In an era of Big Data, critical thinking is arguably more necessary than ever before. Just because you read it on the Internet doesn't mean that it's true.† Consider the following questions:

- What is the data telling us?
- What is the data *not* telling us?
- What happens if we act and we're wrong?
- What happens if we don't act?

❓ TIP

In an era of fake news and alternative facts, critical thinking is more important as ever.‡

Even Agile Analytics Can't Do Everything

Despite myriad claims to the contrary, there's no one secret to building an innovative culture or keeping employees motivated. Sure, countless books and blog posts promise quick fixes (aka *clickbait*). For this, they garner lots of attention, but ultimately the truth is far more nuanced.

Remember the three different types of analytics in Chapter 3. One of them (prescriptive) looks forward and attempts to influence future outcomes. To be sure, adopting Agile methods typically bears fruit earlier than longer Waterfall ones.

Agile methods such as Scrum are just quicker and a better means to the same end: solving business problems. This may entail improving sales, reducing customer churn, and so on. Put differently, don't expect Scrum to guarantee *any* outcome. By itself, it will not correct

---

*For the whole story, see http://econ.st/2e9QuKQ.
† If only a certain politician would realize this. . . .
‡ I would teach this course for free: http://callingbullshit.org.

dysfunctional corporate cultures, nor will it make recalcitrant employees see the errors of their ways.

Agile Analytics Won't Overcome a Fundamentally Bad Idea

Let's say that you run sales at a large car-insurance company. Historically, your company's customer-evaluation model has relied almost exclusively on demographics and other internal data—specifically customer loss histories. Over the last few years, though, you've noticed a change: a growing percentage of customers are not renewing their policies. You want to understand why this is happening.

You start thinking that your longtime model for generating quotes is too simple and decide to scrap it altogether. You believe in the power of data and begin purchasing it from data brokers. You start scraping data from different sites. After all, as Chapter 2 noted, this is easier than ever. In other words, you begin to build a model based largely on external data. Six months later, renewal rates have plummeted even farther and you find yourself out of a job.

It turns out that you were focusing your efforts in the wrong direction. You would have been better served by augmenting your model with credit-score data. For years now, auto insurers have begun incorporating these "behavior-based" data from credit bureaus into their quotes. The rationale is simple: All other things being equal, people who pay their bills on time also tend to be safer drivers.

If it makes you feel any better, at least you have company. No software-development or analytics method would have saved Peeple, the ill-fated and much-maligned "people-rating app." Agile analytics don't turn horrible ideas into sound ones. Ideally, though, they can quickly determine if an idea or direction has merit.

CHAPTER REVIEW AND DISCUSSION QUESTIONS

- What types of people issues can thwart organizations' analytics efforts?
- What types of data issues can do the same?
- What are some of the limitations of Agile analytics?

NEXT

The next chapter briefly looks at the analytics implications of design. As with Nextdoor in Chapter 11, product design directly affects the types of data collected, and by extension, the types of analytics. Companies that take design for granted don't merely run the risk of building an ugly or user-unfriendly app. Chapter 14 shows how the implications of ignoring the data and analytics of good design are hard to overstate.

The Importance of Designing for Data

Lessons from the Upstarts

War is 90 percent information.

—Napoleon Bonaparte

I n April 2013, thousands of doctors, scientists, and researchers from dozens of international organizations did what was once considered a pipedream. Led by the National Human Genome Research Institute and the U.S. Department of Energy, this group of luminaries successfully completed the Human Genome Project.

The potential benefits of this accomplishment are manifold and hard to overstate. Perhaps most important, new testing and related data should enable far better predictions of individual health risks, superior means of alternative medicine, and personalized medicine. The possibilities are endless. As it happens, though, the process of comprehensive mapping of complex attributes at the smallest possible level—and critically, *the relationships among these attributes*—is not restricted to health care.

THE GENES OF MUSIC

In 1999, Will Glaser and Tim Westergren were thinking about a different kind of radio service. What if they could map the "music genome"? If they pulled it off, they could provide remarkably personalized music recommendations. Along with Jon Kraft, the group founded Savage Beast Technologies, the predecessor to the music-streaming service Pandora (launched in January 2000).

At a high level today, there are two ways to provide music over the Internet. Spotify, TIDAL, Google Play Music, and Apple Music all allow their users to select the songs they want to hear. The now-defunct Rdio did the same.* If you want to listen to a single artist, album, genre, or song all day long, then try these music services. Their core assumption is that listeners know exactly what they are in the mood to hear. Why get in their way? Waiting for random songs harkens back to radio's early days; instead, customers should serve as their own DJs.

From the onset, Pandora operated under a fundamentally different premise from many of the other legal on-demand music services yet to come. Pandora's folks saw things much differently. Listeners certainly know the albums, songs, artists, and even genres they *generally* like, but what if they only like what they know? Not all unknowns are created equal. To paraphrase Donald Rumsfeld, there are known unknowns and unknown unknowns. There are things we don't know we don't know. What if Pandora could learn its customers' listening

---

* The company filed for bankruptcy on November 16, 2015.

preferences? What if it could identify interesting music based on detailed listener and song data?

From Theory to Practice

Pandora recognized that one size doesn't fit all, but it needed to do several things to accomplish its ambitious goals. First, to be appreciably different from terrestrial and even nascent Internet radio stations such as AOL Radio, Pandora needed to quickly make *personalized* recommendations—and good ones. Second, it could not rely on simple factors such as a song's genre and the year that it was released. To this end, Westergren and company worked on what it dubbed, and eventually trademarked, as the Music Genome Project.

According to its website, Pandora believes that:

> . . . each individual has a unique relationship with music— no one has tastes that are exactly the same. So delivering a great experience to every listener requires a broad and deep understanding of music.

> Our team of trained musicologists has been listening to music across all genres and decades, including emerging artists and new releases, studying and collecting musical details on every track—450 musical attributes altogether.*

Each song's "gene" corresponds to a very specific characteristic. Examples include:

- The gender of the lead vocalist
- The prevalent use of groove
- The level of distortion on the electric guitar
- The type of background vocals[†]

---

* See www.pandora.com/about/mgp.
† For more on this, see www.pandora.com/corporate/mgp.shtml.

Interestingly, Pandora maps different genres—*and different numbers of genes*—to different music genres. For instance, with more than 400 genes, jazz is far more complicated than rock and pop (150 each). As Rush guitarist Alex Lifeson once famously riffed during a show, "Jazz is . . . weird."

Equipped with this vast trove of data, Pandora could then build its product to reflect its core belief. The service made it easy for users to create their own radio stations by selecting a single artist. The service then dutifully serves up its best guesses—that is, songs that its algorithm believes matches the current artist. This serves as only the starting point. As Figure 14.1 shows, users can vote songs up or down, and skip the recommendation.

Figure 14.1 Example of a Pandora Recommendation: "The King of Sunset Town" by Marillion
Source: Pandora app.

Pandora is intent on learning as much about your music tastes as possible. Pandora's founders correctly believed that even the most hardcore audiophiles couldn't possibly know the name of every song, band, and genre that they would like. There's plenty of vast ocean of *undiscovered* music out there—if people only knew about it. As the following story illustrates, I, for one, am eternally grateful for one of its recommendations.

THANK YOU, PANDORA

Formulaic three-minute, radio-friendly songs in 4/4 time signatures never did it for me. Since I was a kid, I have always preferred a genre of music known as *progressive rock*. Bands born in the 1960s and 1970s such as Rush, Yes, Pink Floyd, and Genesis made the type of bold, complex, thematic, and experimental music that innately appealed to me. Later on, I would come to appreciate the music of Porcupine Tree and Dream Theater. Of course, terrestrial radio stations wouldn't touch most of their songs—some of which exceeded 20 minutes in length in odd time signatures such as 5/4 and 13/8.

In late 2010, I regularly listened to music via iTunes and Pandora. (I have since become a Spotify subscriber.) Back then, iTunes and Pandora could not have been more different. iTunes allowed me to listen to any of the 11,000 songs in my personal library. In other words, these were songs that I *owned*—either because I had burned a CD to my digital library or purchased them via iTunes.

Up until recently, Pandora didn't work that way.* Pandora let users stream hundreds of thousands of songs from its library whether the user owned them or not. If I wanted to dial up a specific track such as Rush's "Working Man," iTunes was the way to go. If I wanted to explore unfamiliar terrain, Pandora was my choice. Maybe Pandora would help me discover other bands writing the types of tunes that appealed to me.

Pandora quickly figured out my music preferences. As expected, the service served up popular prog-rock staples from the 1970s. I wasn't surprised to hear tracks from *The Wall* by Pink Floyd and *Selling England by the Pound* by Genesis. Good stuff to be sure, but I had owned these albums for years and had rocked out to these songs many times before. What bands had I *not* heard before that I would enjoy? What were *my* unknown unknowns? It didn't take long for Pandora to blow my mind.

I started hearing songs from Marillion, an obscure English "neo-prog" band dating back to the late 1970s. I found myself routinely voting "thumbs up" to the Marillion anthem "Sugar Mice" and the incredibly poignant, even ethereal "Neverland." The band's thoughtful lyrics and

---

* In March of 2017, Pandora launched Premium Subscription Tier, an on-demand subscription service meant to challenge Spotify's supremacy.

(*Continued*)

carefully arranged music resonated with me at a visceral level—especially when played live.

It wasn't long before I started gobbling up Marillion's back catalog in earnest. Within a year, I owned each of the band's studio and live albums and the DVDs quickly followed. The question was not Why did I love Marillion's music? Rather, it was How in my musical travels had Marillion escaped me? What took me so long to discover this band?†

In hindsight, although I was late to the Marillion party, I feel right at home. Most fans appreciate the same type of music.

---

† Marillion played seven dates with Rush in 1986. What I wouldn't give to have attended a show!

THE TENSION BETWEEN DATA AND DESIGN

There's always been more than a bit of tension between data folks and their design brethren.* As companies such as Amazon, Facebook, Google, and Yahoo! have discovered, it's not easy to strike the right balance between thoughtful human curation and cold, data-driven algorithms. Facebook learned this lesson with its NewsFeed. (See "Automation: Still the Exception That Proves the Rule" in the Introduction.)

Douglas Bowman is "Internet famous" because of how he reacted to this very tension. The Google designer abruptly quit the search giant in 2009, frustrated with, in his opinion, the company's unhealthy obsession with data. In his words:

> Yes, it's true that a team at Google couldn't decide between two blues, so they're testing 41 shades between each blue to see which one performs better. I had a recent debate over whether a border should be 3, 4 or 5 pixels wide, and was asked to prove my case. I can't operate in an environment like that. I've grown tired of debating

---

*I wrote about this subject for *Wired* in November 2014. See http://tinyurl.com/ztmud3s.

such minuscule design decisions. There are more exciting design problems in this world to tackle.[1]

Since its inception, Google hasn't been the ideal place for design purists—the anti-Apple, if you will. After all, the company has always been all about data. Up until recently, it did not sell any tangible products. Without perhaps the world's largest trove of information, Google might not even exist. You can make the same claim about Facebook. These companies live and die by their data. That's one way to run a business—and today, it's hard to argue with the results of such a data-oriented approach. Of course, not every organization operates under this belief.

Exhibit A: Apple explicitly rejects data-based design. Steve Jobs believed that it was "really hard to design products by focus groups. A lot of times, people don't know what they want until you show it to them."[2] Jobs wasn't alone in his unwavering belief in the primary importance of good design, data be damned. Tim Cook has largely continued his iconic predecessor's design-centric vision. The new head honcho has eschewed using customer data in any way, even when threatened with court orders after the San Bernardino terrorist attacks. (See "The Primacy of Privacy" in Chapter 1.)

All Design Is Not Created Equal

It's disingenuous to frame this argument as "design versus data" or "art versus analytics." This is a false dichotomy. Organizations can get a little bit pregnant; they can use both data *and* design. For instance, consider Netflix. The company uses data and analytics to inform its marketing efforts, but neither drives character and plot development in its original shows.

Directors and actors aren't mindless automatons. If they had to listen to analytics, I suspect that most would respond much like Douglas Bowman did. It's interesting to note that in March 2017 Amazon announced that it was surveying customers to determine which pilots to pick up for the upcoming year.*

---

* See http://bit.ly/2o4MkoG.

Designing a highly technical product or algorithm, though, isn't the same as directing a dramatic series. A painting or a book of poetry is analogous to an airline engine. With regard to the latter, data matter more than ever. Engineers are increasingly using virtual test benches, new data sources, advanced computer simulations, and extremely sophisticated 3D modeling software to build much better mousetraps.

Even a decade ago, engineers designed products that often left a great deal to chance. Thanks to advancements in methods such as computational fluid dynamics and finite element analysis, this is beginning to change. These methods allow engineers to more accurately quantify risk in the prototyping stage. Via superior data and analytics, they are more quickly identifying structural problems. They are translating requirements into computer-generated product models. Innovations such as these are allowing Boeing and Airbus to create more fuel-efficient engines.

 TIP

Design and data aren't natural enemies.

Data and Design Can—Nay, *Should*—Coexist

To be sure, relying too heavily on data and technology minimizes—if not eliminates—human creativity. Objections like these notwithstanding, the next wave of computer-aided design is unfolding before our very eyes. Some of these new technologies are downright fascinating. (Forget airplane engines: computer modeling may change heart surgery as we know it.*)

Getting down to brass tacks: More than ever, data and technology will continue to drive innovation and design improvements. Data may not play a prominent role in your company's next product, but those who ignore recent advancements do so at their own peril. As Nextdoor demonstrates in Chapter 11, intelligent design leads to better data and quicker problem resolution.

---

* See http://bit.ly/2mD0xMp.

CHAPTER REVIEW AND DISCUSSION QUESTIONS

- Go back to 1999 when Pandora was just an ambitious idea. Did its founders insist on mapping each and every song before launching its products? What about each gene of each song? Why or why not?
- Why does Pandora ask new users to enter their birth year, zip code, and gender? What can the company do with this information? What other information would help it better customize its music recommendations?
- Is Pandora finished mapping each song's genes? That is, does the company have the capability to add additional "genes" in the future? Why or why not?
- Do you think that Pandora's recommendation algorithm has changed over time? How so?
- How is technology changing design and data?

NEXT

This book concludes with a look forward. We may not know exactly what's coming, but that doesn't mean that we can't prepare. To paraphrase the iconic Rush song "Tom Sawyer," even if changes are not permanent, change is.

NOTES

1. Douglas Bowman, "Goodbye, Google," *stopdesign*, March 20, 2009, http://tinyurl .com/cga6xe.
2. Owen Linzmayer, "Steve Jobs' Best Quotes Ever," *Wired*, March 29, 2006, http://bit .ly/2q3AoaI.

PART **FIVE**

Conclusions and Next Steps

The final chapter asks some fundamental questions about where we're going and how we plan on getting there.

This part includes the following chapter:

■ **Chapter 15:** What Now?: A Look Forward

What Now?

A Look Forward

With great power goes great responsibility.

—J. Hector Fezandie

More organizations are moving their analytics efforts away from Waterfall to Agile practices. As such, they can expect to encounter a number of enduring challenges as well as some new and especially formidable ones.

This chapter briefly describes some of the biggest obstacles and opportunities that enterprises will face as they remake analytics, try to move more quickly, adopt new methods, and deal with constantly shifting business and tech landscapes.

A TALE OF TWO RETAILERS

Writing for the *New York Times*, Charles Duhigg caused quite the stir in a February 2012 article called "How Companies Learn Your Secrets." Duhigg described how Andrew Pole, a statistician for big-box retailer Target

> was able to identify about 25 products that, when analyzed together, allowed him to assign each shopper a "pregnancy prediction" score. More important, he could also estimate her due date to within a small window, so Target could send coupons timed to very specific stages of her pregnancy.[1]

And the company did just that with astonishing accuracy. Case in point: Target knew that a 16-year-old girl was pregnant before the girl's own father did. After seeing the flyer that Target had mailed his daughter, the father stormed into a store outside of Minneapolis, Minnesota, and demanded to see the manager.

> "My daughter got this in the mail!" he said. "She's still in high school, and you're sending her coupons for baby clothes and cribs? Are you trying to encourage her to get pregnant?"

> The manager didn't have any idea what the man was talking about. He looked at the mailer. Sure enough, it was addressed to the man's daughter and contained advertisements for maternity clothing, nursery furniture and pictures of smiling infants. The manager apologized and then called a few days later to apologize again.

> On the phone, though, the father was somewhat abashed. "I had a talk with my daughter," he said. "It turns out there's been some activities in my house I haven't been completely aware of. She's due in August. I owe you an apology."[2]

Pole wasn't going rogue here. (The statistician was just using many of the methods described in Chapter 2—and then some.) Rather, he was carrying out the wishes of his manager, and presumably, the company's top brass.

Pole couldn't have imagined that the results of his work would go viral, but none of that ultimately mattered. It's no overstatement to label the Target story a PR fiasco for the company. Privacy advocates expressed concern—and this was *before* the company copped to a massive data security breach that affected roughly 40 million customers. Perhaps people will look back at Target as a cautionary tale of how social media can accelerate a salacious story. Target may not have done anything illegal per se, but its actions left many people feeling downright icky.

Before passing judgment on the company and its management, though, take a deep breath and consider the following:

- By no accounts did Target appear to do anything illegal—at least in the United States. Its management merely wanted to market its products as effectively as possible. Doesn't every company do this—or at least try?

- Target competes with Amazon, a company whose founder and CEO once famously said, "Your margin is my opportunity."

- In today's cutthroat retail environment, *showrooming* has become the norm. Customers often find the product they want to buy, and before taking it to the counter, check the Internet to see if they can find it cheaper somewhere else. If the answer is yes, then Retailer A just helped Retailer B book a sale.*

Knowing all this, do you still feel that Target crossed some line? You could make the argument that actions such as these aren't optional; they're usually required, especially for publicly traded companies with fiduciary responsibilities to maximize shareholder value. In this vein, Target faced a great deal of arguably unjustified scrutiny for using data to target its ads (pun intended), something that most companies do—including arguably its main competitor.

---

* Amazon's mobile app scans product bar codes and almost always finds what you're looking for within a few seconds.

Test for Echo

On November 6, 2014, just about everyone's favorite retailer quietly released what now appears to be a revolutionary technology product.* The Amazon Echo home speaker "lives" inside customers' homes and represents a different type of computing interface: voice. Consumers ask Echo questions and it provides answers. Beyond that, Echo instantly provides an increasing array of services and features. (The company's pithy but clever commercials demonstrate its everyday uses.)

Echo does more than tell you the weather—much more. It is an über-smart digital assistant that learns what types of music you like. It lets you request rides via Uber. With your permission, it accesses your calendar and reminds you when it's time to skedaddle. Oh, and via increasingly sophisticated artificial intelligence, it learns your behavior and preferences. Much like Amazon.com's, Echo's recommendations are designed to improve over time.

Analysts expect sales to reach 5 million units by 2018.[3] In effect, Amazon created an entire product category. Google Home launched on November 4, 2016, a full two years after Echo. Expect imitations from Apple, Samsung, and others soon.

To me, the most noteworthy part of the Echo launch is what *didn't* happen. Privacy advocates raised no concerns about such a potentially invasive device. Think about that for a moment. No alarm bells. Just loads of sales and reviews.

The obvious question is Why? Why did a single, *ultimately relevant* Target print ad cause a public backlash? And why did Amazon Echo—an electronic, data-gathering device that becomes intimately familiar with many aspects of customers' lives—just skate by? Perhaps most intriguing of all, what if Target had released an Echo-like device before Amazon?

Squaring the Circle

In a way, it's unfair to compare the two scenarios. Duhigg is an award-winning writer. His article contained all of the elements of a good

---

* As this book was going to print, Amazon announced the new version of Echo. The Echo Show is equipped with a seven-inch screen that plays media, responds to voice commands, and can be used to make video calls.

story: a contemporary theme, a compelling plot and story, inherently believable characters, and a surprise ending to boot. Echo's tale isn't nearly as riveting. I suspect that Amazon would have faced a Target-style backlash if Alexa had, without provocation, asked that same oblivious father in Minnesota if he wanted to buy baby clothes for his upcoming grandchild. (I'd also bet that the people at Amazon who worked on Echo thought of the very same scenario when designing the product.)

At the end of 2016, I had the opportunity to discuss the Target story with Bill Franks, an analytics expert and author. He had graciously agreed to record a 20-minute guest lecture for my Enterprise Analytics class. Franks astutely pointed out that executives ought to ask themselves three questions regarding *any* product, service, or campaign:

1. Is it legal?
2. Is it ethical?
3. Will it upset people if word gets out?

For the first two questions, the answer was no. Target discovered the hard way, however, that a company can pass the first two tests but fail the third.

People weren't upset with Amazon because Echo didn't cross any line. Its launch was anything but a fiasco, and Echo is a very new product. As such, there's nothing for customers to get upset about— *at least not yet.* Who's to say that it won't face a similar crisis at some point? This is a distinct possibility, especially considering that Amazon is actively courting third-party developers via software development kits and application program interfaces.* For years, Amazon has embraced platform thinking, and Echo represents an extension of that core philosophy.

Those significant disclaimers aside, though, Amazon seems robust enough to survive the occasional botched product launch, system outage (such as the one on March 28, 2017), or even minor privacy breach. Since its inception in 1994, Amazon has excelled at building

---

* See https://developer.amazon.com/services-and-apis.

a long-term bond with its customers. Jeff Bezos knows that customer trust is no commodity; it is an incredibly valuable asset and the company has always treated it as such. Brad Stone's *The Everything Store* unearths some fascinating nuggets about the juggernaut. Tellingly, Amazon senior meetings intentionally leave one seat open to remind everyone that the customer is always in the room.

This modus operandi has served Amazon well. It has reaped significant rewards for the intense fealty and trust that it has cultivated—and not just in the form of a steadily increasing stock price. In 2016, the Reputation Institute named it America's most reputable company for the third straight year.*

Amazon's timing couldn't be more propitious. (See the TRUSTe study in "The Primacy of Privacy" in Chapter 1.) As a result, the company today is in a most enviable position: It can do things that most companies simply cannot. Because of its extensive bank of consumer trust, Amazon can act fast and take major risks with minimal reputational damage. Put differently, Amazon is playing a different game than Target, never mind aggressive upstarts such as Uber.

❓TIP

Organizations can learn quite a bit from Amazon when it comes to resolving the tension among speed, privacy, and trust. There's no quick fix. Play the long game.

APPLE-LIKE ISSUES

In December 2016, police discovered a 31-year-old dead in the hot tub of Bentonville, Arkansas, resident James Bates. As CNN reported, "Benton County Prosecuting Attorney Nathan Smith hopes the voice-activated Echo will provide information."[4] Much like Apple did in the San Bernardino terrorism case, Amazon is resisting the prosecutor's requests to obtain the data. Expect many more stories such as these in the future.

---

* See http://bit.ly/2nG1qRb.

THE BLURRY FUTURES OF DATA, ANALYTICS, AND RELATED ISSUES

The law of unintended consequences is alive and well. Just ask execs at Target and Nextdoor. In the case of the latter, even an app designed with noble or benign intentions can ultimately enable undesirable, even illegal, behaviors. Consider the two ends of the data continuum:

- **Unequivocally legal:** Amazon recommends a Stephen King book because similar customers bought the latest from Dean Koontz.

- **Unequivocally illegal:** A hospital's employees carelessly and routinely swap employee and patient data. In so doing, they clearly violate the Health Insurance Portability and Accountability Act. Even worse, that data winds up on black-market websites and the Dark Web.

No one can rightly criticize Amazon and its ilk for such innocuous uses of data. Pandora did the same thing for me by recommending the music of Marillion, and for that I am forever grateful. (See Sidebar "Thank You, Pandora" in Chapter 14.) As for the hospital, no one can plausibly defend its employees' actions. Parenthetically, I can only imagine the reaction in Europe, where privacy regulations far exceed those in the United States.

But what about all of those dicey areas in between these two poles? What about scenarios that lie somewhere in between (1) that which is clearly legal and acceptable, and (2) that which is unequivocally illegal and unacceptable?

Increasingly, our business and political leaders will have to ask these very questions. Organizations must make increasingly difficult and fuzzy judgment calls around data and analytics. Sure, a particular insight or data source may be valuable, but does it run the risk of attracting unanticipated and possibly catastrophic baggage à la Target? This is precisely the question that organizations' data-governance bodies and professionals will need to address.

Data Governance

I've read many descriptions of the term *data governance* over the years, but I'm fond of this simple, 19-word definition:

> The process of creating and agreeing to standards and requirements for the collection, identification, storage, and use of data.[5]

The business case for data governance is straightforward: Firms can avoid finding themselves in hot water for permitting employees to use enterprise data in untoward ways. Data stewards and data-governance councils can be invaluable in this regard. It may sound bureaucratic, but data-governance efforts yield benefits in the form of increased internal controls, reduced risk, greater compliance, and at least some degree of legal protection.

Organizations have historically developed data-governance charters and policies based mostly on what its employees were allowed to do with *internal* data. That is, a firm could decide and strictly "govern" its data and the data-related actions of its workers.

As the examples in this book show, that world has come to an end. For several reasons, classic notions of *data governance* just don't play nicely with Big Data, smartphones, streaming data, and the like. First, no one can make the case that data "born" *outside* of the organization is all noise and no signal. Second, a firm may be able to rigorously govern, manage, and control its enterprise data. The same cannot be said, however, about external data.

❓TIP

Big Data has arrived. In this new world, traditional data governance only offers the illusions of control and predictability.

Agile approaches invalidate neither the importance of data governance nor its general principles. Still, the increased speed, reduced batch size, and an iterative mind-set of the methods that this book describes should give executives pause. It is perilous to assume that the new boss is the same as the new old boss.

Just like their employers, data-governance professionals will need to be more Agile than ever. Expect more situations like Target and Nextdoor in the future. As such, there's never been a greater tension among the needs for speed, effective data governance, and long-term planning. One thing is certain: Organizations will have to make difficult trade-offs. Their customers, users, and the public at large will judge these firms by those trade-offs.

In fact, it's fair to ask the question: Is every employee at least somewhat responsible for data governance today?

❓TIP

Whether they hold formal data-governance responsibilities or not, organizational leaders should pay close attention to the types of things that new analytics and data sources enable.

Data Exhaust

This book began with the story of how Foursquare used check-in data to accurately predict Chipotle's quarterly sales well before the markets and research firms could. In the process, Foursquare may have finally stumbled on a viable, data-driven business model. Put differently, Foursquare is among a growing number of companies to recognize the value and power of digital footprints. This phenomenon also goes by the increasingly popular term of *data exhaust*: "the data generated as a byproduct of [our] online actions and choices."*

Do you think that the data collected by web browsers, smartphones, search engines, and social networks is icky? Remember that many of these applications and services only gather information about us and what we're doing while we *actively* used them. Depending on your individual settings, smartphones and wearable devices may do the same *constantly* and *passively*. As the Internet of Things continues to gain steam, expect more data, more analytics, and more opportunities to use both in fascinating, scary, and even illegal ways.

---

*For more, see http://whatis.techtarget.com/definition/data-exhaust.

It's Complicated: How Ethics, Privacy, and Trust Collide

Against this backdrop, what will firms do? What choices will their leaders make and why? It's clear that governments, the courts, and other social institutions cannot keep up with today's technology, data, and dizzying pace of change.

Consider Uber again. The company conceived of, built, launched, and used God View for months or years before its customers, its "driver-partners," regulators, and media outlets learned of its existence. (See "Uber: The Economist's Dream" in Chapter 1.) Airbnb can skirt city housing ordinances and build a $30 billion business in a remarkably short time. It can then refuse to provide government officials with data that could prove the very legality of its business under the auspices of customer and user privacy.

More than ever, executives seem to use "privacy" alternatively as a sword or a shield, depending on their goals. They can circumvent rules and pay fines if and when they are caught. Alternatively, they can take the high road. As we see from the example of Amazon given earlier in this chapter, organizations can view the status quo as a massive opportunity to build long-term customer trust. In the process, they can differentiate themselves from their competition.

In the original *Jurassic Park*, Dr. Ian Malcolm (portrayed by Jeff Goldblum) gives an ethics lecture, culminating with one of my favorite movie quotes: "Your scientists were so preoccupied with whether or not they could, they didn't stop to think if they should."* Keep that in mind when thinking about contemporary data and analytics, and their privacy and security implications.

FINAL THOUGHTS AND NEXT STEPS

We've reached the end of our journey. We have learned that success with analytics is neither guaranteed nor easy. Generally speaking, though, it stems from specific tools, data sources, and the method employed. While important, these factors tell only a part of the story. Individual, team, and organization mind-sets matter just as much. Put in another way, the soft stuff is just as important as the hard stuff.

---

* Watch it here: http://bit.ly/2nxrZIV.

Admittedly, the people side of the equation is often the trickiest beast to tame. It's often far more difficult than the technical side. Even on an individual level, constantly questioning assumptions and looking outward can be exhausting. Add to the mix team dynamics, communication issues, cultural differences, personality types, external pressures, and organization politics, and it's no wonder that the whole is so often less than the sum of its parts.

Despite these often-formidable obstacles, the benefits of Agile analytics usually justify their costs. As we have seen, they can bear fruit in the form of better models, decisions, and outcomes. Keep this in mind when you encounter new types of data, analytics, tools, challenges, and opportunities in your careers.

CHAPTER REVIEW AND DISCUSSION QUESTIONS

- What happened at Target? Why did the public react so strongly?
- Is every type of data or analytics fair game? Where do you draw the line?
- Why has there yet been no similar backlash with the Amazon Echo?
- Will technology, data, and privacy continue to collide? Why?
- With respect to building trust, what can organizations learn from Amazon?
- What is data governance? Why is it fundamentally harder to pull off today compared to even 15 years ago?
- What is data exhaust? Can you think of other ways in which it might be valuable?

NOTES

1. Charles Duhigg, "How Companies Learn Your Secrets," *New York Times*, February 16, 2012, http://tinyurl.com/83h7t2q.
2. Ibid.
3. Taylor Soper, "Amazon Echo Sales Reach 5M in Two Years, Research Firm Says, as Google Competitor Enters Market," GeekWire, November 21, 2016, http://bit.ly/2iZ8Akg.
4. Eliott C. McLaughlin and Keith Allen, "Alexa, Can You Help with This Murder Case?," CNN, December 28, 2016, https://cnn.it/2iG3oSm.
5. Scott H. Schlesinger, "Making Sense from Nonsense with Data Governance," Data-Informed, January 28, 2015, http://bit.ly/2nzkmEx.

Afterword

To defend what you've written is a sign that you are alive.

—William Zinsser

Thank you for buying *Analytics: The Agile Way*. I hope that the preceding pages provoked you to think about how you and your current or future organization should approach the practice of analytics. Beyond some level of enjoyment and education (always admirable goals in reading a nonfiction book), I also hope that you can apply your newfound knowledge in the workplace, in the classroom, or in both.

And perhaps you are willing to help me. Each of these actions is very valuable:

- Putting the book on the curriculum of a course that you teach or one of your colleagues teaches.

- Writing a review of the book on Amazon.com, BN.com, Goodreads.com, or your blog. The more honest, the better.

- Mentioning the book on your blog, Facebook, Reddit, Twitter, LinkedIn, and other sites you frequent.

- Recommending the book to anyone who might find it interesting.

- Giving the book as a gift.

- Referring the book to people who still work in newspapers, magazines, television, or industry groups. Social media hasn't entirely replaced traditional media.

- Checking out my other books at www.philsimon.com/books.

I don't expect my book to become a bestseller, but stranger things have happened. Case in point: *Capital in the Twenty-First Century* by Thomas Piketty, an obscure French economist. In 2014, the 700-page tome on income inequality became the very definition of a surprise hit. It proved what the physicist Niels Bohr once said: Predictions are difficult, especially about the future.

I'd love to sit at the storied oak table on *Charlie Rose*, but that is exceedingly unlikely to happen. I write books for several reasons. First, that's just what a writer does. Second, I believe that I have something meaningful to say about an important topic. Next, I like writing, editing, crafting a cover, and everything else that goes into publishing books. To paraphrase the title of an album by Geddy Lee, it's my favorite headache. Next, although Kindles, Nooks, and iPads are downright cool, I enjoy holding a physical copy of one of my books in my hands. In our digital world, creating something tangible from scratch just feels good to me. Fifth, I find writing to be incredibly cathartic. Finally, writing books opens doors for me. Case in point: I wouldn't be teaching at ASU's W. P. Carey School of Business if I hadn't started putting my ideas out there.

At the same time, though, producing a quality text takes an enormous amount of time, effort, and money. Every additional copy sold helps make the next one possible.

Thanks again.

Acknowledgments

Kudos to Team Wiley: Sheck Cho, Judy Howarth, Kimberly Monroe-Hill, Barbara Long, and Michael Henton. Additional thanks to Karen Davis, Johnna VanHoose Dinse, Luke Fletcher, and Hope Breeman.

Thank you, Raghu Santanam and all of my colleagues, including Matt Sopha, Rob Hornyak, Alan Simon, Matt McCarthy, Linda Price, Mike Frutiger, Altaf Ahmad, Amy Hillman, Angie Saric, and Hina Arora. Ditto to Zach Scott, Sasha Yotter, and Shannon Bullock.

A tip of the hat to Bob Charette, Terri Griffith, Adam Friedman, Ellen French, Jane Simon, Andrew Botwin, Mark Frank, Thor Sandell, Rob Metting, Melinda Thielbar, Brian and Heather Morgan, Heather Etchings, Michael West, and Marc Paolella. To more than 25 years of friendship, increasingly ugly hoops, and antagonism, this ragtag bunch of misfits: David Sandberg, Michael Viola, Joe Mirza, Chris McGee, and Scott Berkun.

Rush has given me—and so many others—four decades of truly remarkable music. Thank you for such a storied career. Marillion continues to inspire me and give me hope for the future. Ditto for the cast and creative team behind *Better Call Saul*. Thank you for what you do and how you do it.

Finally, thank you to my parents. I'm not here without you.

Selected Bibliography

BOOKS

Alt-Simmons, Rachel. *Agile by Design: An Implementation Guide to Analytic Lifecycle Management*. Hoboken, NJ: John Wiley & Sons, 2015.

Ayres, Ian. *Super Crunchers: Why Thinking-by-Numbers Is the New Way To Be Smart*. New York: Bantam Books, 2008.

Berlin, I., and H. Hardy. *The Hedgehog and the Fox: An Essay on Tolstoy's View of History*, 2nd. ed. Princeton, NJ: Princeton University Press, 2013.

Bilton, Nick. *Hatching Twitter: A True Story of Money, Power, Friendship, and Betrayal*. New York: Portfolio/Penguin, 2014.

Blank, Steve, and Bob Dorf. *The Startup Owner's Manual: The Step-by-Step Guide for Building a Great Company*. Pescadero, CA: K&S Ranch Press, 2012.

Bock, Laszlo. *Work Rules!: Insights from Inside Google That Will Transform How You Live and Lead*. New York: Grand Central Publishing, 2017.

Carr, Nicholas. *The Big Switch: Rewiring the World, from Edison to Google*. New York: W. W. Norton, 2008.

Carr, Nicholas. *The Glass Cage: How Our Computers Are Changing Us*. New York: W. W. Norton, 2015.

Christensen, Clayton. *The Innovator's Dilemma: The Revolutionary Book That Will Change the Way You Do Business*. New York: HarperCollins Publishers, 2003

Collier, Ken. *Agile Analytics: A Value-Driven Approach to Business Intelligence and Data Warehousing*. Boston: Addison-Wesley, 2013.

Croll, Alistair, and Benjamin Yoskovitz. *Lean Analytics: Use Data to Build a Better Startup Faster* (Lean Series). Boston: O'Reilly Media, 2013.

Crow, Michael M., and William B. Dabars. *Designing the New American University*. Baltimore, MD: Johns Hopkins University Press, 2015.

Edwards, Douglas. *I'm Feeling Lucky: The Confessions of Google Employee Number 59*. New York: Mariner Books, 2012.

Fisher, Tony. *The Data Asset: How Smart Companies Govern Their Data for Business Success*. Hoboken, NJ: John Wiley & Sons, 2009.

Franks, Bill. *Taming The Big Data Tidal Wave: Finding Opportunities in Huge Data Streams with Advanced Analytics*. Hoboken, NJ: John Wiley & Sons, 2012.

Franks, Bill. *The Analytics Revolution: How to Improve Your Business by Making Analytics Operational in the Big Data Era*. Hoboken, NJ: John Wiley & Sons, 2014.

Greenwald, Glenn. *No Place to Hide: Edward Snowden, the NSA, and the U.S. Surveillance State*. New York: Henry Holt, 2014.

Gurin, Joel. *Open Data Now: The Secret to Hot Startups, Smart Investing, Savvy Marketing, and Fast Innovation*. New York: McGraw-Hill, 2014.

Isaacson, Walter. *Steve Jobs*. New York: Simon and Schuster, 2011.

Johansson, Frans. *The Medici Effect: Breakthrough Insights at the Intersection of Ideas, Concepts, and Cultures*. Cambridge, MA: Harvard Business School Press, 2006.

Kahneman, Daniel. *Daniel Kahneman*. Cambridge, UK: Cambridge University Press, 2008.

Kim, Gene, and Kevin Behr. *The Phoenix Project: A Novel about IT, DevOps, and Helping Your Business Win*. Portland, OR: IT Revolution Press, 2014.

Leffingwell, Dean. *Agile Software Requirements: Lean Requirements Practices for Teams, Programs, and the Enterprise*. Boston: Addison-Wesley, 2011.

Lewis, Michael. *Moneyball: The Art of Winning an Unfair Game*. New York: W. W. Norton, 2013.

Lewis, Michael. *Flash Boys: A Wall Street Revolt*. New York: W. W. Norton, 2015.

Lindbergh, Ben, and Sam Miller. *The Only Rule Is It Has to Work: Our Wild Experiment Building a New Kind of Baseball Team*. New York: Henry Holt, 2016.

Pariser, Eli. *The Filter Bubble: How the New Personalized Web Is Changing What We Read and How We Think*. London: Penguin, 2012.

Patterson, Scott. *The Quants: How a New Breed of Math Whizzes Conquered Wall Street and Nearly Destroyed It*. New York: Crown Publishing, 2010.

Rico, D. F., H. H. Sayani, and S. Sone. *The Business Value of Agile Software Methods*. Plantation, FL: J. Ross Publishing, 2009.

Ries, Eric. *The Lean Startup*. New York: Crown Publishing, 2014.

Seidman, Dov. *How: Why How We Do Anything Means Everything*. Hoboken, NJ: John Wiley & Sons, 2007.

Silver, Nate. *The Signal and the Noise: Why So Many Predictions Fail—but Some Don't*. New York: Penguin, 2012.

Simon, Phil. *The Next Wave of Technologies: Opportunities in Chaos*. Hoboken, NJ: John Wiley & Sons, 2010.

Simon, Phil. *Why New Systems Fail: An Insider's Guide to Successful IT Projects*, rev. ed. Boston: Cengage Learning, 2011.

Simon, Phil. *Message Not Received: Why Business Communication Is Broken and How to Fix It*. Hoboken, NJ: John Wiley & Sons, 2015.

Sims, Chris, and Hillary Louise Johnson. *The Elements of Scrum*. Foster City, CA: Dymaxicon, 2011.

Stone, Brad. *The Everything Store: Jeff Bezos and the Age of Amazon*. London: Corgi Books, 2014.

Stone, Brad. *The Upstarts: How Uber, Airbnb, and the Killer Companies of the New Silicon Valley Are Changing the World*. Boston: Little Brown, 2017.

Taleb, Nassim Nicholas. *The Black Swan: The Impact of the Highly Improbable*. New York: Random House, 2007.

Tetlock, Philip E. *Expert Political Judgment: How Good Is it? How Can We Know?* Princeton, NJ: Princeton University Press, 2006.

Tetlock, Philip E., and Dan Gardner. *Superforecasting: The Art and Science of Prediction*. New York: Broadway Books, 2016.

Weinberger, David. *Everything Is Miscellaneous: The Power of the New Digital Disorder*. New York: Henry Holt, 2008.

Zinsser, William. *On Writing Well: The Classic Guide to Writing Nonfiction*, 30 Anv. Rep. Ed. New York: HarperCollins, 2006.

ARTICLES AND ESSAYS

Messerli, Franz H. "Chocolate Consumption, Cognitive Function, and Nobel Laureates." *The New England Journal of Medicine* 367 (2012): 1562–1564. www.nejm.org/doi/full/10.1056/NEJMon1211064.

Takeuchi, Hirotaka, and Ikujiro Nonaka. "The New New Product Development Game." *Harvard Business Review*, January 1986.

About the Author

Phil Simon is a sought-after keynote speaker and recognized technology authority. He has written seven other business books, two of which have won awards: *The Age of the Platform* and *Message Not Received*. In the fall of 2016, he joined the faculty at Arizona State University's W. P. Carey School of Business. He teaches courses on system design, enterprise analytics, and business intelligence.

When not speaking, writing, and teaching, Simon advises organizations on analytics, strategy, emerging trends, and management. His contributions have been featured by the *New York Times*, *Wired*, *Harvard Business Review*, CNN, NBC, CNBC, *Inc.* magazine, *BusinessWeek*, the *Huffington Post*, and many other sites. He holds degrees from Carnegie Mellon and Cornell University.

Simon's website is www.philsimon.com. Find him on Twitter at @philsimon.

Index